TYORKIN & THE STOVEMAKERS

Alexander Tvardovsky

TYORKIN & THE STOVEMAKERS

poetry and prose by
Alexander Tvardovsky

translated from the Russian by
Anthony Rudolf

introduced by
C. P. Snow

TRANSLATIONS
A CARCANET PRESS PUBLICATION

Copyright © Anthony Rudolf 1974 (Translations)
Copyright © C. P. Snow 1974 (Introduction)

SBN 85635 066 4

All rights reserved

First published 1974
by Carcanet Press Limited
266 Councillor Lane
Cheadle Hulme, Cheadle
Cheshire SK8 5PN

No part of this publication may be reproduced or transmitted in any form or by any means, electronic or mechanical, without permission in writing from the publisher except by a reviewer who wishes to quote brief passages in connection with a review for inclusion in a magazine, newspaper, or broadcast.

Printed in Great Britain
by W & J Mackay Limited, Chatham

CONTENTS

7   INTRODUCTION *by C. P. Snow*

17 TRANSLATOR'S NOTE

FROM *Vasily Tyorkin*
19 Na Privale / During the Halt [last part]
20 Pered Boyem / Before Battle
27 O Nagrade / About Medals
29 V Nastooplenii / In Attack
34 Smert i Vaeen / Death and the Soldier
41 Tyorkin Pishet / Tyorkin Writes

FROM *Tyorkin in the Other World*
44 'Let us repeat: in the prime of his life . . .'
45 'It's well known you won't miss your curls if . . .'

48 *The Stovemakers*

INTRODUCTION

TVARDOVSKY came to London for the first and only time early in 1960. He was accompanying Konstantin Aleksandrich Fedin, the head of the Writers' Union, on an official visit, and the two of them called on us soon after they arrived. I hadn't met either before, and all I knew of Tvardovsky was that he had great popularity as a poet in the Soviet Union (I still hadn't much idea how great), and that he was the editor of *Novy Mir*. At that time we were living in a largish old-fashioned ground floor flat at the Earls Court end of Cromwell Road, which later became one of the subjects about which Tvardovsky teased me.

Fedin, being the senior, was installed in our best drawing-room chair. In his courteous, amiable manner, he introduced his companion, who sat on the sofa alongside my wife. For a long time, Tvardovsky said nothing at all. I was talking to Fedin and there was the usual Anglo-Russian palaver about what, if anything, they would drink. It was around eleven o'clock on a London winter morning, Cromwell Road outside was not a specially exhilarating prospect, and I felt that a drink or two would cheer us all up. However, Fedin, who is an abstemious man and who anyway wasn't well, wouldn't drink anything: and Tvardovsky, who I later discovered was not abstemious by any standards, had made a self-denying ordinance for the duration of the trip, which was to be a fortnight. This was a common precaution of Russians at that period. They weren't sure how their drinking habits would appear to Western eyes, and were sometimes relieved to find that the English weren't a nation of teetotallers. Finally Tvardovsky was persuaded to accept a maidenly glass of sherry but remained silent. The rest of us were speaking about the Soviet writers we had read, and the English writers they had read. In the fifties, the interchange had been small and we were making pious resolutions to increase it. The conversation was civil and sensible enough, but scarcely gripping. Then I mentioned a couple of Russian contemporaries. The large form on the sofa stirred, and Tvardovsky said: 'Even in a socialist society, it is difficult to remove all inequalities in talent.'

It was said completely deadpan, without expression. For the first time, I had a good look at him. He was a big man, about six feet, heavy with bone and muscle. He had a face which couldn't have been anything but Slav, broad, capable of much mobility, eyes a very light, transparent blue. In that, as in everything else, he was Russian of the Russians. A cowlick of hair usually fell across his forehead. It was a good face, clever, humorous, often difficult to read.

He had enormous hands. When we knew each other well, he used to say: 'Look at them. They are four times the size of yours, Charlie. Peasant's hands. They are part of my stock-in-trade. Whatever else people say, they can't say I'm not a peasant. I'm the only one who is.' By this he meant that nearly all the eminent Soviet writers of his generation came from various sorts of professional origin. For some ideologues, that was a disconcerting truth. It was also true that Tvardovsky came from the aboriginal peasantry. He was born, in 1910, in Smolensk province, not even in a village, but in a tiny crossroads settlement of a few izbas, where his father was acting as blacksmith, and had his patch of land.

After his first remark, Tvardovsky began to talk. I asked about the Tyorkin poems, which I then knew only by hearsay: had they been translated anywhere in the West? No, he said, with feeling. He spoke about Russian reputations in England, and English reputations in the Soviet Union. He was very funny, both then and nearly every time I met him afterwards. He was humorous as well as witty, with the Russian blend of humour and wit which is much like our own, except that perhaps it sometimes shows more extravagant swings of mood than are common with us. Tvardovsky was a strong and tough-minded man, but I have seen him pass, still funny, from elation to abandoned gloom in the same five minutes.

I met him several times during his London trip, and took to calling him Sasha. Aleksandr Trofimovitch was rather too much of a mouthful, and Sasha was the ordinary diminutive. Not to be outdone, he must have found out what was the diminutive of Charles, and thereafter, believing in perfect symmetry in all human interchanges, always called me Charlie. He was the only human soul who has ever addressed me by that appellation. He also wanted to satisfy his curiosity, or his suspiciousness, of which he possessed a share. I had talked to him about nineteenth-century Russian literature, which happened to have been a passion of mine since I was a very young man. I knew a bit more of writers less well-known in the West, Shchedrin, Leskov, Ostrovsky, the radical critics, than most Englishmen would be likely to. Tvardovsky tracked me down at an official party and got me alone in a corner. Had I really read anything by Belinsky, or Chernishevsky? Or Nekrasov? What did I know about them? He seemed to be moderately satisfied by my replies.

A few months later, my wife and I were making one of our visits to Moscow. That was the midsummer of 1960, and it happened to be a somewhat delicate period in Anglo-Soviet relations. Not that that was unusual, but we were a trifle speculative about what our reception would be. The Paris Conference had broken down in disorder a day or two before, and Pasternak had just died. As we descended over the airport (that was before Sheremetyevo was in operation, and landings were a good deal more casual), one of the pilots pointed out of the window and told me: 'Comrade

Tvardovsky is waiting for you on the tarmac.' The pilot was excited. This was a great man down below. Incidentally, it was unusual to use the style Comrade to a foreigner. For the first time anywhere, I was being presented with someone who possessed literary fame as Dickens might have known it.

There were a number of acquaintances to meet us. Then there was a long wait in the lounge: not because of the formalities, because those were as usual brushed aside, but because mysteriously our bags didn't appear. Affable conversation about books and appointments (no reference to tender topics, all as matey as ever), but no bags. Also no drink, which at that airport seemed also to have disappeared. A. A. Surkov, then Secretary of the Writers' Union, went off to investigate. Tvardovsky said: 'Aleksei Aleksé'ich [Surkov] is making a noble oration about the necessity of getting you into Moscow quickly. He is a man of great and noble eloquence. It will take much longer.'

Those two were friends. Personal relations among Soviet writers were often nothing like what the West imagines. Nor, incidentally, were literary and other sympathies.

I saw a good deal of Tvardovsky in Moscow that time, and on each subsequent visit, until he became seriously ill, which happened a couple of years before he died. I had great affection and admiration for him, and learned some simple things and some rather more complicated. The most important thing, and one which hasn't been clearly realized in the West, which always watches Soviet literature through political eyes, at least as much as they do ours, was that he was first and foremost a poet. That was what mattered to him by far the most. He had a proper pride in his achievement, and it was his greatest joy.

As a consequence, one of his greatest disappointments was not to be recognized for his poetry in the Western world. This was a peculiar chagrin, when he was so much the most popular poet in his own country. I will say a little more about his work shortly: but it is essential to realize that, even in the Soviet Union, where the tradition of poetry hasn't had the discontinuities of the West, and where taste is much more eclectic, he was working in an idiom which everyone down to the simplest could understand. A poet as admirable as Pasternak, deeply Western-influenced, wasn't: nor are such poets as, say, Vosnesensky. A very approximate equivalent over here to Tvardovsky might be John Betjeman – but a John Betjeman using themes which could be understood, not primarily by the suburban middle-class, but by the Saturday afternoon football crowds, or almost anyone capable of reading. As a result, his circulation was, and remains, enormous. Editions of volumes of poetry in the Soviet Union are very large, by our standards. A poet beginning to be known would have a *tirage* of perhaps 50,000: one already established, such as Sokolov or

Evtushenko, more like 100,000. Tvardovsky's editions ran into the millions. Photographs and TV don't spread faces round the country in the U.S.S.R. as continuously as here, but his was as familiar as a film-star's. One could see glances turned towards him whenever he walked along a Moscow street. There weren't many writers in the world – perhaps there were none – who were greeted by their own people with such obvious love.

He was a public figure, and he took his responsibility seriously. I can give no authority except my own impressions for what I am going to say. We became friends and had a number of intimate discussions – in his Moscow flat, in the *Novy Mir* office, and in his dacha out at Pakhra. The way in which we each lived was, incidentally, a subject which he never lost interest in. I once thoughtlessly observed that I lived very simply. Great roars of laughter. His friend and neighbour Tendryakov, a fine writer, was present. 'Charlie has an apartment of *ten* rooms.' That was the old flat in Cromwell Road, where we had first met, and which he had carefully surveyed. Well, the facts were true enough, his own flat in Moscow had perhaps four rooms, which was lavish in the early sixties. And yet – the dacha at Pakhra, where this conversation took place over a gigantic meal, was not the ordinary wooden summer cottage, but more like a substantial red-brick house at Barnet, with a sumptuous bathroom, standing in an acre of so of ground. 'I am a peasant. I must have my own piece of land.' In a good many ways, I insisted, he lived more opulently than I did, though he wasn't a materialistic man, except that he liked his food and drink.

He was a public figure. He had been editor of *Novy Mir* in the early fifties, displaced for some years, and then reinstated as the editor, which he remained until he was displaced again, about a year before his death. The West insisted on regarding this as the important, the only important, feature of his life. It was certainly important to many Soviet writers. It was through him, and through him alone, that *A Day in the Life of Ivan Denisovitch* was published. He had influence with Khrushchev, who admired him: and the book, of course, fitted some of Khrushchev's policy. Tvardovsky tried to publish *The Cancer Ward*. He was cunning, brave and patient about publishing many other literary works, less controversial than Solzhenitsyn's, but in Soviet terms only slightly less. He did all this in what he conceived as the line of duty. Nevertheless, it was second, as it would be to any genuine writer, to his own creative work. The bitterest remark I ever heard him utter – and, as well as having a humorous and ironic tongue he sometimes had a bitter one – was in the *Novy Mir* office, surrounded by several of his colleagues. 'I find that in your country [to me] I am known as an *editor*. In my wildest dreams I could never have expected that.'

That brings me to his attitudes. So far as I can trust my judgement, there were three which counted – apart from his poetry and his family affections, which affected him as they would any of us. He was – and this was the deepest of all – a passionately patriotic Russian, with an attachment to the Russian land, the Russian people, the Russian language, which was more intense, emotional or even sensual, than any Westerner can easily comprehend, though perhaps our ancestors could. Then he was a liberal. But he was also a Communist. Being a liberal Communist is not an easy fate, but both parts of that description have to be given their proper consideration. He was a member of the Central Committee of the Party for years. He believed that the regime was the only possible one for his country. He wanted, however, to improve it. That was where his liberalism came in. Crimes had happened which must never happen again. He was the last man to be deceived or comforted by phrases like 'the cult of personality'. Those features of the system which had made such crimes possible must be studied and rooted out. He had a little influence, and it was his responsibility to use it.

I don't remember many discussions on the economical and practical aspects, the bread and butter, of the Soviet socialist system. I have a faint memory that, like other liberal Communists, he suspected that a tincture of mixed economy was the most satisfying arrangement for everyone: but he wasn't profoundly interested, so long as the country was strong and gradually the hardship eased. As I have mentioned, he wasn't a materialistic man. Civilized nations didn't depend on lashings of consumer goods. One could make do and put up with things. In this he was like many other Russians. If they had been as materialistic as Anglo-Saxons, the Soviet Union would have provided more creature comforts by this time.

So far as Tvardovsky had a hankering after a dilution of the centralized economy, it wasn't for practical reasons at all, but because this appeared to make life more spiritually liberal. He wanted to preserve the great virtues of his own people and society: at the same time he was affected by the *esprit* of, not so much Westerners, but Hungarians and Poles, who aren't without influence in Soviet intellectual circles. Some degree of constraint, some response or at least sensitivity to public opinion, could give strength to art, particularly literature, the one he understood best. Too much constraint, excessive response, took away its fibre. Tvardovsky understood both those propositions as well as any man alive, and, all through his career as a public man of letters, he was steering his way between them.

That was not only the problem of a liberal Communist. It was the problem of a serious man anywhere. For instance, Tvardovsky had no doubt that Soviet literature would benefit from a greater degree of sexual clarity (curiously enough, there never has been much in Russian literature, except for the work of a few proto-writers who amused Pushkin and his circle of Petersburg aesthetes, beginning in the early 1800s). Just as strongly, Tvardovsky had no doubt that the total permissiveness of the West was self-destructive. No literature could live long in that fashion. 'Your nineteenth-century writing may have been suitable for ladies' ears, Charlie, but it was a damn sight better than what your people are writing now.' I don't think I have ever met a Russian, except maybe a hundred per cent dissident, who believed in unqualified sexual liberty in literature. Tvardovsky didn't. He wanted more than Soviet writers have at present (even now, it varies a lot among the Republics – some modern Armenian writers, for example, are pretty uninhibited), but he thought one had to invent a kind of case law, one had to play it by ear.

In any event, that wasn't a major issue. Increased political liberty in literature really was. That was what his official struggles were about. Once again, he may not have believed in, or wanted, unqualified political liberty. Of this I can't be sure. He probably had too much of the traditional Russian reverence for the written word, and faith in its effectiveness, for that. We haven't much reverence for the written word, and no faith whatever in its effectiveness, so it comes easy to us to let people write what they like and pay no attention to them afterwards. The price of total freedom is total neglect. That offhand indifference has never come naturally to Russians, and doesn't do so now.

Tvardovsky had about as much faith in the therapeutic side of literature as his opponents had in its subversive one. He not only believed that *Denisovitch* was a major work of literary art: he believed that it would be a major influence in cleaning up the society. (Of course, his most conscientious opponents, who never denied the talent of the work, believed just as passionately that it would do social harm.) He was certain that the Stalin period would never be understood, or its lessons learned, until there was unqualified freedom to discuss every last piece of suffering. He approved of Thomas Hardy's lines: 'Who holds that if way to the Better there be, It exacts a full look at the Worst.' There he couldn't make any kind of compromise in belief. He was absolute and committed.

That was the hard core of his liberal stand. On other things he just wanted an element of sense. His daughter studied art, but he was not as far as I could gather a specially visual person. Still, he knew about Kandinsky, Lessitsky, Malevitch. He knew that they were regarded as among the most significant figures in the century's painting, and that official Soviet painters were jeered at. How political was all this? The one obvious conclusion was, contemporary Moscow ought to be able to see the abstract paintings, there ought to be something like a gallery of modern art.

He took the same view – this also is not uncommon among liberal Communists – about religious expression. I haven't seen the text of Solzhenitsyn's funeral speech, but the extracts which appeared in the Western press, and some of Solzhenitsyn's behaviour, may lead people here astray about Tvardovsky. In the shots shown in London, Solzhenitsyn was crossing himself as fervently as at an Orthodox service. It is, of course, known that he is a devout believer, and that his model for the future of his country would be something like a Social Democratic state under the leadership of, or at least closely associated with, the Orthodox Church. Uninformed persons may have imagined that this was Tvardovsky's model too. That would be utterly wrong.

Tvardovsky, as I have stated, was a Communist. He may have respected Solzhenitsyn's social dreams, but even that, from all the evidence, seems doubtful. He would certainly have thought them unrealistic, and probably undesirable. Further, he didn't share – and on this subject I am not guessing – Solzhenitsyn's religious beliefs. Tvardovsky was not a Christian, or a religious believer of any kind. Like many men of feeling, he remembered the church services which he attended as a child. He had precisely the sort of affection for them that I myself have for those of the Anglican church – and he believed as little. He had a nostalgic tenderness for old Russia, if you like: the kind of emotion that leads hard-baked Russian officials to talk of Novgorod, Pskov, Rostov the Great, as *real* Russia: the kind of emotion that bursts out of Simenov's famous war poem, 'Do you remember, Alyosha, the roads behind Smolensk?' (The poem goes on to speak of the simple Christian graves of their forefathers.) It is an unjustifiable softening and sentimentalizing of Tvardovsky, however, to think that such emotions, which in our own fashion many of us have, affected his mature convictions. He was an honest and rooted man. He stood like a rock, exceptionally subtle in his emotional nature, strong and simple in his intellect; it is very wrong to distort it.

I want to repeat what I have already said. It is important for Western readers to grasp, among the complexities of East-West cultural politics, one simple point. Tvardovsky's real significance in Russian literature rests on the long connected cycle of poems in which the central figure is Vasily Tyorkin. By the side of that, anything else he did or anything else he wrote, in verse or prose (he wrote very little prose, and sometimes one regrets it, when one enjoys the engaging short story translated here, almost his only exercise in prose fiction), is minor. *Tyorkin* is his masterpiece. It is our loss that to understand it requires from English readers two different efforts of imagination, neither of them easy.

First, as I have mentioned, he wrote these poems for an artistic purpose, and in a form, which are no longer easily assimilable by us. We have to try to read *Tyorkin* as our ancestors read *Don Juan* or *The Rape of the Lock*. The second comparison is perhaps a shade nearer the truth. Tvardovsky was working, like Pope, within the discipline of a very strict form. Within that discipline he had, like Pope again, a remarkable verbal inventiveness. Variety of intonation, wit in the Popish sense and also in our own – and, what Pope didn't have, methods of revealing an abnormally strong, delicate and humorous human understanding. That is, he could, as no twentieth-century Western poet would be able to, naturally and unselfconsciously write an epic cycle and convey what a Western writer would attempt only in a novel.

Samuel Marshak, one of the most gifted and successful of modern translators (his Russian Burns ranks with those great translations which may be rather better than the originals), was one of Tvardovsky's greatest admirers. I once saw an essay of his in which he analysed some of the internal subtleties (verbal, assonantal, rhythmic, psychological) of passages from *Tyorkin*. How to suggest these in English? English has plenty of words, just about as many as Russian. That was no problem. But with Tvardovsky, far more, perversely, than with apparently esoteric poets such as Pasternak, the absence of inflections in English was a real problem, though not the only one. What had great diversity and subtle charm in Russian would come out mechanical or wooden in English, as Pushkin has always done. Marshak saw this very clearly, but he didn't see anything like a satisfactory answer.

Mr Rudolf has found a bold answer of his own. He has deliberately broken up the strict form. He has used many kinds of device to give an approximation to what is carried in the Tvardovsky line. With much cunning and literary tact, he has, in the verse translation itself, insinuated information which would be unfamiliar to most Western readers and would otherwise require sheafs of footnotes. (*Tyorkin* is packed with references, not exactly private jokes, but jokes which have different levels of meaning for sophisticated readers – some of which, incidentally, must have eluded millions of Tvardovsky's audience in the Soviet Union.)

My feeling, for what it is worth, is that Mr Rudolf has achieved some considerable successes in these translations. It will be fascinating to see what their impact is on English readers who come completely fresh to Tvardovsky, or have heard of him only through journalistic stereotypes. For me, a good deal of the wit comes through, and the deep, affectionate, very Russian fellow-feeling: some, though not all, of the humour: a fair amount of the narrative skill. The chief loss, I fancy, is the psychological insight which is there unstressed in Tvardovsky all the time. It may be uncapturable.

The second major effort of the imagination needed from Western readers isn't linguistic, or technical, or even literary in a narrow sense at all, but quite as difficult. *Tyorkin* is essentially a war epic. War means something different to Tvardovsky, and to all Russians of his generation, from what it does to us. It is primal. It is a collective experience so profound that nothing compares. The Russians have fought two great wars, one in 1812, one in 1941–5. They have forgotten neither, and can't forget. It is not trivial that they call the second the Great Patriotic War. Patriotism to Tvardovsky, liberal as he was inside his own society, was a major virtue. Unless we understand that, we understand nothing about him – or, I think, about much of the Soviet Union today. And so, of course, he, again like most Russians, revered the military virtues. Courage, duty, sacrifice, loyalty to one's comrades – one didn't argue about them, they were necessary and good. Don't tell me that he needed instructing about the horrors of war. Like a number of Russian writers, he was a war correspondent right through from 1941–5. The Russian officer casualties were very high, and many of these correspondents, being educated men and having picked up military experience along the way, had to become improvised commanders. That happened to him. He had seen the devastation of his own beloved Smolensk countryside (there are many allusions in *Tyorkin*), he had seen more corpses and scraps of corpses than most men. That didn't prevent him reverencing the military virtues.

It would have been quite impossible for him to tolerate our frivolity on the subject. He wasn't easily shocked, but he would have been shocked by *Oh What a Lovely War*. He admired English literature (which most Russians do), he rather liked England (which most Russians don't), but he would have thought that that was the expression of a country in advanced decline.

So *Tyorkin* is something like a great novel about war and must be read as such. Much of it was actually written in wartime, and there are indications that Tvardovsky sometimes subdued his criticism and his pyschological realism. The wonder is that he subdued them so little. *Tyorkin* is the incarnation of the Russian private soldier (Russian in the full sense: he is a peasant from the Smolensk region), and has been accepted as that in the Soviet Union for a generation. Tvardovsky treats him with love, but often with quite remarkable candour. At times Tyorkin bears a certain family resemblance to *The Good Soldier Schweik*. Tyorkin is pretty good at scrounging and swinging the lead. He wouldn't be as good as his German opposite number in that war if he had to improvise. He learns to be brave, but that doesn't come quickly (Tvardovsky had deep insight into how men can behave bravely without it being first nature). He loves the Russian land, and is instinctively patriotic (Tvardovsky couldn't have imagined anything else, but he doesn't make this sentimental in Tyorkin). He loves life, and doesn't want to die.

The most recent opinion of *Tyorkin* that I have seen comes from a Russian near-contemporary of Tvardovsky's. Konstantin Simenov has written a trilogy of novels about the Soviet-German war which have had great and deserved success in his own country, and are well known here. He has been reflecting on Russian war literature which, certainly in quantity, probably in quality, is more substantial than that of any country. Perhaps I should interject that Simenov isn't given to exaggerated praise of anything or anyone. What are the great peaks in that war literature? he was asking. Only two. *War and Peace, hors concours* beyond doubt. The other peak? Tvardovsky's *Tyorkin*.

C. P. Snow

TRANSLATOR'S NOTE

Even outside the Soviet Union Alexander Tvardovsky is honoured as a great creative editor. And rightly. But Tvardovsky saw himself as, and wished to be remembered as, a poet. I would like briefly to discuss certain points arising from the actual business of translating the extracts from his two epic poems 'Vasily Tyorkin' and 'Tyorkin in the Other World', and the long short story 'The Stovemakers'. With regard to the story, I have occasionally adapted an idiom or made explicit something that is implicit in the original, in order to clarify what might be obscure to an English reader and at the same time to avoid recourse to footnotes.

The translator of poetry should always attempt to describe what he has attempted to do, and why. 'Vasily Tyorkin' is a very long, often informal and occasionally rambling epic ballad. There are irregularities in rhyme, metre, diction, structure and syntax. In a letter to a Czech student dated 19 June 1962 and published in May 1973 in *Druzhba Narodov* (the Organ of the Union of Writers in Moscow), Tvardovsky states that to translate him (i.e. Tvardovsky) is very difficult because he often deviates from literary norms and because his verse line is deceptively simple in its adherence to spoken rhythms.

These days it is well understood that even a tightly structured short lyric must not, cannot be translated 'literally', or rather – to put it more positively – you have to translate *everything*, every dimension of the total structure. As Tvardovsky says in the letter quoted earlier: 'Only a free translation can be exact – a literal translation can never be exact *in the essentials*' (my italics). In other words, the unit(y) is the poem not the word or the line. What is true of a tight little lyric is *a fortiori* true of a 'Vasily Tyorkin', and I have not hesitated to change (i.e. *trans-late*, bring across) all aspects of the original, taking it apart in order to put it together again as an English poem. In any case, as Tvardovsky says in that same letter: 'In my opinion . . . and in the opinion of our greatest masters of artistic translation – with Marshak at the head – a knowledge of the original language is of course necessary for the translator, but even more important is a knowledge of his own language.' For example, and *pace* recent statements by Brodsky concerning the use of rhyme in Hayward's and Kunitz's translation of Akhmatova, Tvardovsky's loose and often expedient rhymes and half-rhymes must not and cannot be dogmatically aped in our uninflected language, but should be loosely and expediently put across as befits the movement and echo of an English ballad in 1974. The story must be kept moving for English readers, and Tvardovsky, a deeply intelligent poet and critic, would have been the first to agree. He would certainly have not expected *slavish* adherence to his metres.

Let me end with an interesting quotation from that sensible letter of 19 June 1962: 'To be translated (and not spoiled!) from Russian into another language is a piece of great and rare good fortune for which you could wait for ever. What can I say about us mortals when, as I well know, even Pushkin still has no Marshak (I have in mind his congenial translations of Burns) either in French or English or German?'

It is a pleasure to acknowledge here some friends who gave me useful advice. First, Heather Maisner, Donald Rayfield and Daniel Weissbort. Then, in particular, Bernard Johnson whose advice concerning 'The Stovemakers' was invaluable and who helped me in the difficult task of selecting passages from 'Vasily Tyorkin' though the final responsibility is, of course, mine. And, above all, Sue Knight, whose knowledge and understanding were always available to me as I was translating 'Vasily Tyorkin'. A big hug for her from the eponymous hero. Finally, affectionate thanks to Brenda Rudolf, Val Warner, and Michael Schmidt for their support.

Anthony Rudolf
January 1974

From Vasily Tyorkin

Na Privale/During the Halt [*last part*]

What kind of man is Tyorkin?
Let us put it plainly:
An ordinary sort of chap,
Everyman's kith and kin.
Still, he is a capital
Fellow. You'll always find
In every company, each platoon
At least one of his kind.

So that you'll know his strongest points
Let us put it plainly:
He isn't well endowed
With beauty in his joints.
He isn't tall, he isn't short,
But he is a real hero.
He fought on the Karelian front
Beyond the River Sestra.

And we do not know why
(We're not inclined to pry) –
Why on that occasion
They didn't decorate him.

Let us – out of politeness –
Not ask why he was missed.
Maybe they misprinted his
Name on the honours list!

Don't look for what's not on a chest:
Just keep eyes front – march two abreast!

Up the line from June,
In battle from July,
Tyorkin once again
Is playing war's old tune.

It's clear to me no bomb or bullet
Has got *my* name engraved upon it!
A scratch from a splinter in battle
Healed up neatly, like a treat!
Three times I was surrounded –
Three times (three times!) escaped unwounded.

And though it was pretty dire
I remained alive
Under parabolas – direct and slanting –
Under three-layered fire!

Often on the weary way
Part of me was scattered, lost
By the roadside, in the dust
Of the men who march away.

All the same,
The cocksparrow's still game!
From the kitchen straight away
To battle: he smokes, he drinks and eats
With relish, no matter how or where he sits.

However cruel, however hard,
Don't give in, keep marching forward.

This is the preamble:
The story will be told.

Pered Boyem/Before Battle

And now I shall report in brief
How it happened – on account
Of war – we made our way up from the rear,
From the German side, to the front.

From the German, from the far side
Of the river, as they say,
Following Soviet power and the front
Our Tyorkin made his way . . .

20

Brother soldiers, thin and hungry –
Though they'd lost communication
With their unit – made their way
In platoons and companies,
Sometimes grouping freely, often
Lonely as sore thumbs –

Our fellow soldiers walking
Through fields, along the edge of woods,
Did their best to be unseen,
With gasmasks for their knapsacks
Entered villages at dark.

Grizzled, with a few days' growth
Of beard they wend their heavy way.
They drop in at any old
Hut and hang around the door
Like men guilty of some crime.
They have no other choice at such a time.

In accordance with the bitter
Custom that honour dictates,
First they beg a drop of water
And afterwards a bite to eat.

Auntie – how can she refuse?
Whate'er you are, you're one of ours.
She won't say a thing to you
But sobs and sobs and murmurs as
She gives you something for your kit.
– God grant that you may come back . . .

Great sadness came over us then
As we dragged ourselves along
Eastwards; barefoot and bone-
thin to regions cold, unknown.
What's there? Where does Russia end?
How far do her boundaries extend?

And yet they made their way. I too.

Along the hateful road I went –
Not alone – we were ten, we
Had a commander too. He
Had worked his way up through the ranks.
Businesslike he was, efficient,
Knew the area round about. More
Ideologically aware myself,
I served there
As a sort of political instructor.

The soldiers followed us. Behind
We left the captured land.
I kept reiterating one
Slogan: Don't lose heart!

Don't overdo it, we'll break through.
No doubt we will survive, so look alive!
The time will come – we shall be back.
What we gave up – we will get back!

If they had asked me to my face,
I knew no more than they
What's there. Where does Russia end?
How far do her boundaries extend?

Sullen, gloomy, our commander
Strode along. Out of the corner
Of my eye, I see he's brooding.
'Stop thinking,' I say.
I speak to him frankly.
Suddenly he asks me in reply,
'My village is just off this road.
What do you think of that, instructor?'
What could I say? 'What do I think?'
I saw him lower his eyes.
He wilted. His moustaches drooped.
What crime was he guilty of –
That his village was so near?
That his soul began to pine?
'It doesn't matter about rules –
Let's call in, if you agree.'

This bright falcon flapped his wings,
Stopped brooding and began to sing
And kept up such a gruelling pace
We dropped behind, as in a race.
But later on we made it and
By the back ways, through the hemp fields
Warily he led the band
To the village, to his home.

That's how it is with soldiers
In war: you fall
On home, creep along by the wall
And drop in for an hour.

Know beforehand there's small virtue
To be gained from your old armchair.
War has dropped in even there
Well in advance of you.
And your being home on leave
Doesn't gladden your
Dearest little woman's heart.
You ran there, slept in fits and starts,
And hurried off again to war.

Master sits down, takes off his shoes,
Puts his right hand on the table
As if he's just come back from the stable,
From the fields, for a snooze.
Like that . . . but it's all different . . .

'Well, wife, heat up the stove a bit!
Supply the company with something hot,
Some rations – everything you've got.'

The children sleep. The wife is quick
This bitterly sad holiday.
However short night is, she has
To share it with the company.

Efficient with the stove, she cooks
At speed, she fries and bakes.
As if we were guests, she spreads

A table cloth, embroidered
With a cockerel or another bird.

She sets out hot food and drinks,
Then beds us down for forty winks,
Looks after us with such concern,
With something like a mother's love,
As though we were the latest
Of a long string of visitors,
As though we were the greatest
Conquering heroes of our time.

Our host himself, the senior
Soldier sitting with his guests,
Has hardly ever in his life
So delighted in his wife.

She could never have been sweeter,
More considerate in her ways,
Than she was at this brief meeting,
On *real* holidays.

How he suffered, this good honest
Fellow and father. He guessed
He was leaving his kids and wife
To an unsure fate, a captive life.

Finishing the drink and parley
The soldiers kip around the house.
The master lies down, but his spouse
Does not come to him early.

The plates clink softly. Then she sews
Beside the fire. The master
Waits, waits in his corner
Over there.
          I feel out of place.

The comrades doze like logs
But I can't get to sleep.
Let me be a sentry, keep
Guard, napping like a dog!

I remove my overcoat
And (as the saying goes)
Make myself a sort of bed
And lie on it: it covers my toes;
Mattress, and pillow for my head.

    Ah, government issue, cloth the best,
        Military overcoat,
    Burnt through by camp-fires in the forest,
        Noble overcoat!

    Famous coat, shot through, threadbare and
        Damaged by enemy fire,
    Yet mended by my own bare hands,
        You're dearer than desire!

    Should you fall mown down by lead, please note,
        Wounded brother, they'll
    Trundle you off in your well-worn overcoat
        To the field-hospital.

    But if you're killed, then your cadaver
        With others in a row, they'll keep
    Covered with your shabby over-
        Coat. So, soldier, sleep!

    Sleep, soldier. For the length of your brief life
        Neither at home nor in the highway's dust
    Have you slept the sleep of the just,
        Whether by yourself or with your wife.

The master comes out on the porch.
I won't forget that night.

'What do you want?'
'I've come to chop some wood for my wife.'

So, the master could not sleep –
As if, at home, he were at war.
He strides to the woodpile,

Chops the brushwood in the moonlight,
Chops and chops and chops till daylight:
For this soldier, brief is night.
It's clear he's worried for his wife –
He loves her. But he does not know
How to help her. Chops and chops.
At dawn the soldier leaves his house.

And the children wake at daybreak,
Look around – their father's come . . .
Look around – strange soldiers,
Various slings and rifles, and
The children, like old adults,
Seem to understand.

Then the children started crying
And I could not help reflecting
That today perhaps the Germans
Armed with rifles would burst in . . .

To this day the children's weeping
In the dawn of that bad day
From the German side, the far side
Of the river follows me.

On the morning of the battle
I could not dream of glory.
All I wished for on the right bank
Was to emerge alive.
Reader, I'll be frank:
Should I ever go back there
I've in mind to knock
At that housewife's door
And beg a drop of water –
Not that I might sit at table,
But so that I can bow
Before that good and simple woman.

Should she ask about her husband,
'I expect he's alive and well.'
And take the axe, remove my coat,
And chop wood for the housewife's stove.

Because the lord and master
Never said a word to us,
Maybe now he warms the earth
He defended like a Tartar.

Still, there're other things to think about.
Brothers, we must hurry on,
Beat the Germans and their sort –
That's what Tyorkin should report.

O Nagrade/About Medals

No, you fellows, I'm not proud.
I needn't guess too far ahead
To say: what do *I* need
An order for? I'll be content
With a decoration. Even that
I'm in no hurry for.
Better have done with the war,
Take home leave on our own side.
Will I still be kicking then?
Hardly likely. Here you fight
Instead of guessing, wrong or right.
But I'll say (getting back
To decorations): that's when
It ought to be presented: coming home.
It should be guaranteed,
And I deserve it.
You all should understand:
It's a very simple matter.
A man comes home from war –
Imagine! I leave our tiny station
For the village Soviet.
I arrive and hope to find
A party. No. Well, never mind.
I go to the next collective farm,
And then a third. My eyes explore
The whole landscape. I knock at every door.
Somewhere in some Soviet
I'll light upon a party yet!

And emerging from the crowd
(Despite the fact that I'm not proud)
I will not roll and light
The usual shag, oh no! I'll
Take out a chic brand, smooth and good,
And, listen boys, I'll sit down there
In just the place I hid
My bare feet as a lad
Under the bench. And I
Will puff away at my cigarette,
Invite those standing by to taste
The luxury. And at my leisure
I'll take their questions on with pleasure.

'Well, what happened?' – 'We saw it all.'
'Must have been hard.' – 'Yes, sometimes.'
'Did you attack them many times?'
'Well, now and again, from time to time.'

Amid the festive noise
The girls forget the other boys.
To every word I say they cling –
I tell them how my rifle sling
Would creak. And then I joke with them.
And there would be one who . . .
At such a moment, friends, you
Know what you can do with your decorations!

See the girl, almost in torment,
Longs for a glance from you, your each
And every word. At such a moment
A medal's not so bad,
When at a party a lad
Is with a girl, a real peach.

No, said Vasily Tyorkin,
And sighed. And again, no, lads.
What use is an order then?
Not looking too far ahead,
I'll settle for a simple medal.
As I told you, I'm not proud . . .

*

Tyorkin, Tyorkin's a good lad.
Try to tell what's happy from what's sad.
Friend, you must have guessed a lot,
Peered at the future – why not?

The leaves fell, and then buds began;
The buds turned into leaves once more . . .
But the post won't carry letters
To your native Smolensk region.

Where are the parties, where the girls,
Where is your village Soviet?
You yourself, Vasily Tyorkin,
Know there's no open road there *yet*.

There is no road, you have no right
To see the village of your birth.
The terrible and bloody fight
Continues, not for glory's sake
But for the sake of life on earth.

V Nastooplenii/In Attack

They'd lived so long in fortified
Defences that already from
The front line even the horses
Knew the way, as in the village
Back to the watercourses.

Along the whole defence-line and
In the forests they called home,
The homely barking of a band
Of small dogs echoed in dug-outs.

Splendidly habituated
The cockerel – those were the days –
Roused the Div. C. always
On time, like a household's head.

And to celebrate the winter
In the baths! – don't spare the steam –

With birch twigs they had inter-
Twined, the soldiers beat themselves.

Between charges, as if encamped, they
Rested idly in a sort of leisure,
Lived, read *Tyorkin* for pleasure –
When suddenly: an order to obey . . .

Sudden order, end of halt
And already eyes advance
Over the abandoned dug-outs, then
Lonely puffs of smoke on the horizon.

And it seems completely normal
That a whole year has gone by
Like a day. The war and all
The like will pass away.

And my soldier, who is greying,
If he comes out safe and sound,
Will recall the fight for Moscow
Was the true battle-ground.

And with a hero's sadness
He'll tell his tale again
While his grandchildren, listless,
Hold his walking stick, his hands . . .

It's difficult to know.
With old folk, we're not always kind.
We'll see when the time comes.
Meanwhile – there's still long ways to go.

*

The battle's in full swing. The grey
Snow is clouded with blue haze.
Up the line Vasily sways
Under fire . . . to his village.

So right to the paternal hearth
In his village, he went that day,

Because the path ran through
The village, not the other way.

What can you do? Some other man
Might find an easier, roundabout
Route, avoiding home. Another might
Offer to cross a steppe that's vast and strange
Or some unknown mountain range.

Whistling soft above your cap
Death will make a man bend low.
The line advances, as if to stop
Something in the field of snow.

And for the youngest soldiers who
Go into the attack for the first time
It is a comfort to know
That Tyorkin is there too.

It's good – although you'll be
Trembling beneath the fire –
To show yourself in front of him
And not be backward in this mire.

No matter that at anguished moments,
As the shells take running jumps,
Hurtling himself as a stone in snow,
Tyorkin like you awaits a lull;

That he, who many times has risked
His destiny and happiness,
On battlefields sometimes has less
Power over his fear;

That maybe this strange fear
Bore away from war
A man who could be spared to stay
In safety to this day –

To this little furrow here
Where, holding his stomach in

He lies, covered with a thin
Human skin. He lies and waits while we're . . .

Somewhere beyond the battlefield
Thinking his own thoughts, he goes –
His pocket-watch will regulate
All time in time of war.

On all explosions his sharp eye
Is fixed, fixed on gaps in the smoke.
He decides the how and why,
This sovereign of the battle-yoke.

Somewhere on the sandy steep
In his dug-out quick with sand
The general looks hard at his map,
Takes out his watch, then slams the lid
Like a trap. Raises his cap
And wipes the sweat from his forehead . . .

Waiting's over, Tyorkin hears:
Platoon! For Russia! Attack!

Although he's read these words –
The war cry on the brink of death –
A hundred times in newspapers,
Has often heard them in the war,
They enter in his soul once more
With the old power of holy writ,
Of sweetest bitterness and truth,
With that unfailing force which leads
Men by hundreds into fire
And takes upon itself a sacred trust.
Platoon! For Russia! Forward! Attack!

The cavalry lieutenant who
Has lost his horse in battle,
Dandified, mustachioed,
Like a schoolboy, on the road
Joking, dancing, daredevil,
Is the first to get up, firing
As he goes. He runs ahead

With the platoon. They go round
The village from the rear. His tracks
Can be seen ahead of all
The others on the snowy ground.

Already here, at the last hut
He lifts his hand to his moustache:
'Well done, lads! Forward!' Dash-
ingly like Chapaev he shouted.
Only, suddenly, he fell
Forward, stumbling, running pell-
Mell. The clear-drawn tracks he cut
In snow were interrupted . . .

And he dived into the snow
As into water, like a lad
From a boat into a weir. And the word
Travelled up the line that
The Commander was hit.

Wounded! As they ran towards him
(For this his name will live)
He raised himself. 'Attack! Ahead!
I am not wounded. I am – dead . . .'

Edge of village, gardens, backyards –
Within easy reach, almost to hand . . .
Tyorkin saw and understood
It was his turn to lead the van.

Platoon! For Russia! Attack!

He signalled, and they trusted him.
Hurrying behind their friend,
Not an instant holding back,
Forty soldiers threw themselves
As one man into the attack.

If the battle turns out well
When it's over, all will tell
In turn, with highest praise, of what
The other comrades gave and got.

'The tanks were victorious.'
'The sappers were glorious.'
'Into the artillery's face
No mud was flung, and no disgrace.'

'But the infantry!'
'In unison they went in.'
'Well what of it?'
'And the air force!'

In a word, simply, *great*.

And it happens too, let's face it,
That success bedazzles.
So many heroes are begotten,
A single one can be forgotten.

Exemplary in his precision,
The general, for order's sake,
Wanted an immediate admission:
Who was the first to break
Into the village? They make
The usual report. Old so-and-so was
First to take it, they said.
But he could not appear in person because
He was seriously wounded.

Then of all the surnames spoken
And, in fact, the first names too,
Tyorkin! burst forth, *Vasily Tyorkin!*
Vasily! The man was you!

Smert i Vaeen/Death and the Soldier

Beyond the hillocks, in the distance
The heat of battle had receded.
On the snow Vasily Tyorkin
Lay alone, unheeded.

Beneath him, soaked in blood, the snow
Froze into a mess of ice.

He heard Death breathe on his brow,
Say, 'Soldier, come with me.

'I am now your lady-friend. I'll
Not take you far. In a white
Blizzard, a white snow fall,
I'll sweep your footprints out.'

Vasily Tyorkin shuddered,
Freezing on his snowy bed.
'I didn't call you, Squinting One,
I am alive, not dead.'

Laughing, Death stooped closer,
Whispering, 'Enough, enough, my brave!
I'm not stupid. I'm not blind.
You've one foot in the grave!

'With the shade of death I touched,
As I went by, your cheek and brow.
You did not sense – how could you – that
It veiled them in a film of snow.

'Do not fear my darkness. Come what may,
Night, believe me, is no worse than day . . .'

'But what precisely are you after?
Do you want *me*, a wounded soldier?'

Death, as though taken aback,
Leant away from him. 'I need
Such a paltry, tiny thing. Indeed
The merest trifle's what I lack.

'Just one sign of consent
That you are sick and tired of life,
That you're praying for the advent
Of Death, your second wife . . .'

'You want *me* to give a sign?'
Death hesitated – thought –

Said, 'Not much to it.
Give a sign and be at rest.'
'No. Allow me, life's worth more
Than rest for us below.'
'Don't barter with me, dearest.
No matter what you say, you wane.'
Death fluttered to his shoulder.
'No matter what you say, your lips are taut,
Your teeth are growing colder.'
'I'm not prone to fright.
I don't choose to go.'

'Look, night's forecast by this cold breeze.
The sunset burns to frost. I'm tougher
Than you. I'm for *now*. You won't freeze
For nothing. It's quicker if you choose.'
'I'll suffer.'

'Are you stupid?' Death retorted.
'You sprawl there contorted.
With a sheepskin I could cover
Pain at once, and keep you warm for ever.
I see that you believe me!
You are weeping. I'm already
Dearer to you.' 'You lie –
It's not because you pity me.
The frost has made me cry.'

'Whether it's happiness or pain –
It's all the same. The cold is cruel.
The ground wind has begun to still
The field. Your friends won't find Tyorkin.
And if you are picked up, what good
Will that do, eh? You would
Lament you had not died
Here, with no fuss, in peace.'

'You're joking, Death, you weave a snare . . .'
He could hardly move his shoulder.
'I haven't even lived yet. I've
One wish only: to survive.'

'Well, if you got up, there would be
Little point,' continued Death.
She smiled. 'You get up, and once again
There's cold, filth, terror and exhaustion.

'Well! Wouldn't that be lovely,
Chum! Consider, in your
Perfect simplicity.'
'Why consider? One doesn't get in war
Any compensation . . . more's the pity . . .
From the courts . . . – But anguish in addition:
How're things at home? my family?
First I'll fulfil my mission –
Finish off the Boche as fast
As possible, then home at last!'

'O.K., You win on that score: duty.
Put why return to your village?
The earth's stripped bare, and pillage
Has left it unfit even for the plough.
All's derelict, both house and field.'

'I'm a worker.
I'll investigate the matter
At home.'
'Your home's destroyed!'
'I'm a carpenter as well.'
'There is no stove.'
'And a stovemaker . . .
I'm a jack-of-all-trades out of
Boredom.
If I live, what's mine is mine.'

'Let an old woman have her say:
What if suddenly, one day,
You're sent home with one arm, or half
A leg? You would soon hate yourself.'

And now it was beyond
The fighting powers of the man
To argue. He saw his blood leak out.
Numb he was at fall of night.

'I have to make just one condition –
Listen, Death, I've no objection . . .'

And exhausted by a cruel
Anguish, lone and weak and small,
He entreating, not reproachful,
Tried to make a deal.
'I'm not worse and I'm not better
Because I'll perish in the war.
But listen, when the whole thing's over,
Will you let me go on furlough
For a single day? Will you let me
On that last day of festival,
Of universal celebration,
Hear the salute of victory
Resounding over Moscow?

That day, will you let me wander
Among the living, just a little?
Let me tap at one small window
In my corner of our country?

And when they come out on the porch
Will you let me light the torch
Of one more little word, O Death?
Half a word?'
         'No, not the breath
Of a syllable!' Death said.
Frozen to his snowy bed

Tyorkin shuddered. 'Then clear out
Of here, Squinty. There's no doubt
I'm still a living man, not dead.

I'll howl with pain, and weep and moan,
And I will perish in the field
Without a trace. But of my own
Free will to you I'll never yield.'

'Wait a moment. I shall find
A better reason. Give me, give me

Just one sign!'
              'Stop! See those men!
They come, they search for me behind,
Before, all round, everywhere.
Soon I'll be in Moscow!
They're from the field hospital!'
'Where are they, fool?'
'Look – just over there
On the snow-bound path!'
Death laughs her head off.
'From the burial squad!'
'But they are living folk, by God!'

Two men trudge up, scuffling snow.
A crow-bar knocks his shoulder-blade.
'One more soldier; I'm afraid
We won't be done by nightfall.
What a day – we're played out
As it is. Here's this lad's
Tobacco-pouch, my countrymen. We need
A smoke – it's the best brand!
Sit down on this stiff . . .

'Oh, if only we'd a kettle
Of hot soup, before we light up . . .
If only there were one little
Drop in the flask – that would be enough.
If only one drop of the stuff
Or two . . .' At this, though he was weak,
Tyorkin did his best to speak.
'Drive off that old hag!
For today at least I'm still alive!'

They turn around and ask, 'What thing
Is this!' They see a soldier, living.

'What do you think of that!
I'll be damned. Well, give a hand –
Let's shift him to the field hospital.'

'Well, it's a most unusual thing.'
Unhurried, they discuss it.

'A body's just a thing.
But here's a body and a soul!
There's hardly any soul
In this body . . . no joke,
It's completely frozen.
In actual fact, we wanted
(No impertinence intended)
To take you to the People's Farm
Where they sow bodies in neat rows!'

'Don't harp on it. The lad's been waiting
Ages. Lift him from the ice.
Carve out his great-coat in one slice.'
But Death said, 'Notwithstanding,
I shall follow on behind.
These countrymen, they are
Designed for a different kind
Of work. You'll carry him quite far,'
She thinks, 'then jolt him. I am patient.'

Two spades, two straps and two over-
Coats across, to make a stretcher.
'Be careful with the soldier, soldier.
Heave ho! Bear up, my friend.'

They struggle to cushion each jolt,
Somehow to smooth out the ride.
'Carry him gently!' He felt
Death follow near on the windward side.

But the road is not a road:
Virgin soil – the snow's waist high.
'You should rest a little, lads.'

'Dear fellow,' says the wise
And mellow countryman,
'Don't worry, don't be sad.
We're carrying a *living* load –
Half the weight of a dead lad.'

The other said, 'That's true –
But all the same, I say

That the living always go
Forward, while the dead
Display their final home
No matter where you carry them.
It's simply a matter of habit.'
They rested silently for a moment.

'Bare hands? My friend, you'll get frost-bite!
Take my hand-warmed mitten – for tonight.'

These goings-on Death watched intently,
And suddenly she thought,
'So, these living folk are friendly
Among themselves, to this degree.
Even when you're dealing with one man,
You've got to reckon with this comradeship.
War! Unwillingly you have to grant reprieve.'

Sighing, Death fell far behind that day.

Tyorkin Pishet/Tyorkin Writes

At last I can inform you, friends,
From bed in hospital,
That Tyorkin, lover of life,
Survived!

And though my sides are sore
From lying like a log,
They say my new leg will be more
Efficient than the one I had before.

And I intend again
– Quite soon, without a cane –
To trample on the grass,
A two-footed man!

At this moment I'm concerned
With one thing only: to return
To my unit speedily,
And nowhere else. I'm lonely.

I lived and fought with unit lads,
Worked hard at my course of studies.
In retreat we soldiers swallowed
Common dust; advancing, our boots
Wallowed in snow. Meanwhile the unit
Is for me, a soldier, everything
On earth, all that I command –
My family and my native land
And home.

My chief wish is (with grateful thanks
To the staff for their speedy ways)
To wedge myself into the ranks
And wait until the better days
Arrive, to walk triumphant in my own Smolensk
And march as far as the border.

However, that's not the heart
Of what I have to say. I'll speak
Plainly: if we must break
Camp and march to another part
Of Russia, I'll be there, wherever
Our great unit's sent to serve.

If a bullet for the third time
Pecks me to Death (that evil Death),
Then, among my comrades I'm
Eager to draw my final breath.

And yet, let's not begin
Hurrying towards that end!
I love life, you know,
Once before I told you so.

And since I'm hurrying
To get back to you,
I'm writing to the general
To tell what I've told you.
I expect the excellent old fellow
Will agree – he gave me a medal
Once – he'll remember me.

He'll waive red tape. Behind
This letter, I hope you'll find
Myself – yes – look!
A special greeting for the cook!

Let him cook as he knows how,
Spice the rations good and rich,
So the ladle will stand upright
Like mad Uzbek Colonel 'Mitch'.

Now I want to tether
My words to this last thought:
I can smell great battles
A mile off, like the weather.

As stallions anticipate
The day for mounting on their mate,
So I can sense the great day when
I rise without a stick again!

And now I'll sleep well, wait to hear.
I've told you all I know, and more!

I embrace you, devils,
                      your kin
And kith, Vasily Tyorkin.

(1941–5)

From Tyorkin in the Other World

Let us repeat: in the prime of his life
And at the height of his powers,
By accident Vasily Tyorkin
Entered the world that's not ours.

He looked around, and what did he see:
Passages warm and light
Like the Moscow Metro, but the arches
Were at a lower height.

The ceiling was thrice reinforced
And he was safe and sound
Even from the devil's bombardment –
Like being underground.

(A bomb! Tyorkin contemplating
The shelter overhead
Couldn't know it all boiled down to *the sort*
Of bomb you had, instead.

That with scientific advances
Today's bomb hurled
Means, if you please, you weren't safe
Even in the other world.)

And now – was it real or a dream –
Tyorkin was not sure,
He saw with his felt boots he was
Leaving foot-marks by the door.

Order everywhere, and cleanness,
Not a fag-end in sight,
Afraid and unthinking the soldier sighed
'This is culture all right'.

It would be great if winter quarters
Were like this everywhere.
Now it is time to get our bearings –
Let's have a look round here.

An arrow for 'entrance' but none for 'exit'
It is quite clear suggests
The warmest welcome, but return
Forbidden to all the guests.

All right, so this is the way things are,
There is always a first
Time; if we could only find somewhere
A drink to quench our thirst.

His throat was terribly parched from the
Unfamiliar heat.
Well, suffer for a while, there's nothing
New about this state.

At this moment the lad sees trains
Approach their destination,
Entering from pre-eternal haze
The final station.

*

It's well known you won't miss your curls if
Someone has cut off your head.
'I have somewhere to get to. O.K.
Make it snappy, and go ahead.'

Since this was how things were going,
Not of his own free will,
Tyorkin sought just a corner
To rest in that gloomy vale.

He'd never slept enough on earth, now
Even if he had to keep
His clothes on, he would rest in warmth, why
Here one is allowed to sleep.

Eternal peace, those well-known words,
They are not spoken in jest.
Whatever we may want, we'll gladly settle
For *one night* of rest.

Forward to distant eternity
Stretch the corridors –
They are the other world's highway,
Above it: semaphores.

And visible for miles so that
You do not go astray,
Are indicators, pointers and
Captions to guide your way.

The harshness of light from the street lamps,
The dryness in the air,
And doors, countless doors, what doors,
Doors, doors everywhere!

All solid and all soundproofed by
Some clever boffin
They stick out from the walls like per-
Pendicular coffins.

Whichever one you opened you
Were met by one hell
Of a powerful and dusty
Damp, sepulchral smell.

On the faces of those sitting there
Looking just like men
The important look means 'I'm not here
Nor back till who knows when.'

He wondered where to start and what
He should be looking for,
'Private. Director's office' said
The sign above the door.

What to do? In the end he screwed
His courage up. Smiling
He entered, saw the counter where
A dead man was busy filing.

Said Tyorkin, I'm registered with you
In the eternal reserve,
As long as I am here, a bed
At least is what I deserve.

(published 1963)

THE STOVEMAKERS

Ever since my childhood I have known about the stovemakers and their peculiar craft, which from olden times has had a shade of mystery, almost sorcery, about it; but I must admit that my knowledge derives more from stories, legends and tales of all kinds than from personal recollection.

In the district where I was born and grew up there was a stovemaker whose fame had spread far and wide. We called him Mishechka despite his venerable age, possibly on account of his diminutive size, although it was quite normal for us to apply diminutives to adults and even to old men: Mishechka instead of Mihail, Grishechka instead of Grigori, Yurochka instead of Yuri. . . .

Among other things, Mishechka was famous for eating clay. I had seen this with my own eyes when he was re-setting the burned-through bottom of our stove. Carefully kneading the clay with his feet in warm water, until it shone like butter, he scooped up a fair-sized piece with his finger, guided it into his cheek, chewed it and swallowed it, all the time smiling like an artist who wishes to show that the performance of his trick presents no difficulty whatsoever for him. I remember very distinctly how Mishechka climbed into our stove, sitting beneath its low arches with his legs spread out like a fork, and how he pricked out the old brick flooring with a special hammer. But how he squeezed himself in there – though small he was not that small – I had no idea. One winter I had a cold, and my grandmother tried to cure it by steam, but I was so cramped, hot and frightened inside the stove that I yelled and shrieked and jerked myself free, and almost fell off the ledge on to the floor.

Now I understand that Mishechka's harmless device of eating clay in front of everyone was one way of showing off his exceptional professional skills – 'Look', it said, 'Not everyone can do this, not everyone can build a stove.'

But Mishechka, like the good spirit of ancient stories, was kind and inoffensive and never used the opportunities inherent in his craft to cause harm to people. Because there were indeed stovemakers who caused their clients plenty of worry and inconvenience if the latter displeased them in some way. For example the neck of a bottle would be fastened somewhere in the chimney flue – and the stove would sing in all kinds of dejected voices, heralding trouble and misfortune for the household. Or a brick would be hung in a certain place from a thin piece of string, calculated to survive the first trial heating of the stove. Everything would be all right until the second or third day, when the string would burn through, and the brick would fall and close the chimney; it would be impossible to light the stove, and impossible to understand why without pulling it apart and building it again.

And there were other tricks of a similar kind. Besides, stoves of the same design differed in the way they heated up, gave off heat, and in their longevity. Therefore traditionally our folk held stovemakers in high esteem, feared them and placated them. One must also take into account the large place, literally and figuratively, occupied by the stove in the life of peasants in the old days. It was not only the source of warmth, not only the kitchen, but also the bakery, universal airing-cupboard and bath-house, and laundry and, finally, the favoured place for a snooze after a day spent working in the cold, after a journey, or simply to cure illnesses and minor ailments. In a word, a good stove meant home. I have reached that conclusion all on my own, and recently I have thought so much and so deeply about stoves and stovemakers that I could write a research paper on the topic.

I had been assigned living quarters across the road from the school. It was a peasant cottage, attached to two similar cottages, where other teachers lived. The cottage was partitioned into two rooms, and the partition came just in the middle of the big double stove, which served in the front room as a cooking-range and in the other as a powerful tiled stove of the Dutch kind. And it was this stove that for a long time caused me extreme depression, misery and on occasion absolute despair. In the classroom or anywhere, alone or with people, whatever I might be doing, I had only to think of the house and that stove, and I would feel that my thoughts were becoming confused, that I could not concentrate on anything, that I was becoming unhappy and embittered.

It was very difficult, almost impossible, to light that stove. The cooking side of the stove did burn somehow, but it did not have much meaning for me, living for the time being without my family. But as soon as we ventured to light the 'Dutch' stove, to warm up the back room where I worked and slept, we had to open the casement windows and doors to let out the smoke which began to fill the whole house, as in a badly ventilated bath-house. I set about lighting the stove myself, but the same thing happened to me. Smoke poured out of the door, out of the ash-pit, oozed out of imperceptible cracks above the stove and made its way out of the rings on the cooking-range in the front room. Each time you'd have thought that people had forgotten to open the flue.

To kindle this stove a great number of devices were resorted to, including the skills and wealth of experience of people who looked after at least ten school stoves in working order.

The caretaker Ivanovna and her husband the one-legged Fyodor

Matveyev were real masters of the craft. Furthermore, each had a system or method, directly opposed to the other's, but equally conducive to good results. Briefly, one could say that Ivanovna began with fire but Matveyev began with wood. I learned these two methods equally well. Ivanovna, an agile and efficient little woman, used to light in the empty stove a piece of birch bark curled like a pipe, a small handful of shavings, a scrap of newspaper or some thin splinters of wood, and by increasing the amount and size of the chips and splinters, she would raise a strong and lively flame to which it was only necessary to add logs and more logs until the wood, penetrated from within by the flames, was jammed so close to the arches that there was no more room to shove a log in.

Fyodor Matveyev on the other hand – partly as a result of being disabled – slowly and carefully arranged the wood in the stove first, in the form of an ordinary cage, or cross-shaped, or vertically, or like a little hut. Deliberately and carefully he would select the logs, always as if he were solving some difficult problem of design. And only after all this would he set fire to the structure, using birch-bark, shavings or newspaper. And he was no less successful than Ivanovna. The stove heated up quickly, the wood burned evenly, there was never a hint of charcoal fumes, and their stoves never cooled down earlier than they were supposed to. But my stove gave equally bad results, whichever method was used.

I began quite seriously to think that maybe some kind of bad joke had been built into it – like the masters of the art used to play in the old days.

Having run into this misfortune, I gradually found out the whole history of the ill-fated stove. It turned out that because of it no one wanted to live in this house. The history-teacher, Maria Fyodorovna, had, I was told, suffered it for a while, then fled. In the summer Ksenia Arkadievna, the maths teacher, had lived there while the adjoining house was being fitted up, but towards autumn she moved in before the decorators had completed their work.

The stove had been constructed by German prisoners-of-war, and after that twice re-set by different amateur stovemakers, but always without success. It was plainly awkward for me to raise with the headmaster the question of repairing the stove once more. But somehow or other it would have to be done again, and this time it would have to be successful.

There was in the whole neighbourhood, I was told, one man, Yegor Yakovlevich, who could build a stove guaranteed to work, but of late he had been taking on such work with the utmost reluctance. He lived off his pension as a former railway employee; he had his house, his allotment, his garden; 'don't want to', and that was that. We sent him a note via his grandson in the 4th class, but he did not deign to answer. Fyodor Matveyev went to see him once, and another time met him somewhere in the village.

But he was ill or he had taken on a job in another village and anything else, well, he said, we'll see.

But further delay was out of the question. The holidays celebrating the October Revolution had passed, and I would soon have to face the winter. Already I was only able to sleep in my room as a result of habits acquired at the front-line; and I corrected the children's dictations and compositions in the staff-room when the other teachers had gone home. On top of everything, I feared that despite my firm warnings my wife Lyolya might turn up unexpectedly with our five-month-old son before I could get the place in some semblance of order.

All these considerations, decisions and delays completely exhausted me. It was not only the stove itself that tormented me, but also the fact that it was an object of conversation, concern, plans and assumptions among all the teachers, the caretakers, the headmaster and, I was certain, the pupils too. Children always know everything about our lives outside school. Even now, when this whole trifling story with the stove is old hat, I feel that I am not telling it with the lightness of touch appropriate to a funny incident but with an anxiety and seriousness that the whole affair, of course, scarcely merits. But ask anyone, particularly a housewife dependent on stove-heating, to what extent a bad stove influences her moods, affects her everyday life and her capacity for work, and she will tell you that a stove like that would make her an old woman before her time. And anyway I had to look at the mishaps with this stove through the eyes of my wife Lyola, a town woman, and also an inexperienced young matron, who would have to live with me in this house.

One morning I woke earlier than usual because of the light reflected from the snow that had fallen in the night, and a clear, simple and it seemed very reliable solution came to me as though with the light.

I remembered the district military commandant, a major whom I had met and talked with when I had called there to register as an Officer in the Reserve. Fool! Go to him. He'll help. He had only to look in his card index and see which of his reservists was down as a stovemaker, and there was my man.

The major received me in his tiny office, just like a garret with three beamed walls and a fourth planked one as a barrier separating him from the rest of the large room.

His unpretentious worried face, with wrinkles on the forehead creasing from his eyebrows to his thick black hair making his forehead appear narrow and giving him an apparently fierce expression, this face took on a sympathetic appearance.

'What can I tell you,' he began, lighting a cigarette. 'Stovemakers. I don't get many of them. A cobbler, a smith. Well, that's another matter.

But a stovemaker.' Suddenly he smiled, baring his big tobacco-stained teeth and his broad-edged upper gums. 'Every soldier is his own stovemaker. Let's have a look.'

There proved to be some stovemakers but one of them was an invalid with only one arm, one of them lived in a remote corner of the district, a third was the chairman of a large collective farm – no use turning to them; and the fourth had been born in 1926: a stovemaker ought to be older than that, the major said. And there were other candidates whom we rejected for one reason or another.

'I'll tell you what,' advised the major towards the end, when he was well acquainted with my story. 'You go and see that wonder-working wizard, Yegor Yakovlevich personally. I've also heard he is an uncommonly good craftsman. Go and talk to him. And if it doesn't work out, come back and we'll think up something else.' He smiled his toothy smile again, slowly covering his mouth with his hand, as people, especially women, do who have lost some front teeth.

His final suggestion, for all his sympathy, seemed to me just words, non-committal politeness.

The next day I made my way to Yegor Yakovlevich along the muddy slippery path which bordered the main road and along which the village straggled. The snow had fallen on the unfrozen earth, and was only to be seen now in gardens and front-yards where no one had walked.

It was early morning, and not many people were out on the streets. I was glad. I didn't want anyone to see me and know where I was going, and why. At that moment I had the sensation that I was wearing tight boots that were causing me a lot of pain, that I was doing my best to hide the fact, but that everyone could see and knew about my misfortune, that they pitied me and also laughed at me a bit. More than anything I can't stand being an object of pity and amusement. And I think this sensitiveness has increased since I became a married man and the head of a family; when I was single it was no problem.

Now, walking along, I thought that everyone – the old woman in rubber-boots at the well, the girl carrying a loaf of bread under her arm and chewing the makeweight, the two boys greeting me at the crossroads – not only knew that I had recently married, was inexperienced and lacked confidence in arranging domestic affairs, but also, if you please, that my mother-in-law, a town doctor and a fine-looking woman, still young, who did not find it easy to admit she was a grandmother, did not treat me very respectfully, and that I felt either shy or afraid in her presence. And that when we had been living in her flat, Lyolya and I and the baby had the smaller room and she had the larger self-contained room, and had to go through ours to get to it.

I had little faith in a successful outcome, having earlier formed a picture of this man as one burdened with the ailments attendant on old age and not particularly interested in earning money. There is nothing worse than asking someone to do something he doesn't want to do or simply need not do.

I made my way down a sloping, well-trodden and dirty path, and walked by a wooden fence which now and then I had to grip to prevent myself falling; then entering a gate I went up to the glazed veranda of Yegor Yakovlevich's little house.

The veranda door was locked. Through the window I could see piles of cabbage-heads, beetroots and carrots with the tops cut off. A long stern face with a weak and limpid beard appeared at one window and a hand gestured that I should go round the other side of the house. I went round, and went up some muddy little steps from the open porch into a passage and, out of politeness, knocked at the heavy door which was padded out with rags.

'Come on, come on,' a hoarse but fairly powerful voice answered from within. 'Don't push it! Pull!'

I entered a very spacious kitchen with two windows. By the right-hand window sat an old man at the table, not an old man but a man of considerable years with a long stern unhealthy sallow face and a sparse straw-coloured – once red – beard mingled with grey. On the table were a samovar, the remains, apparently, of yesterday's meal, and an empty half-litre bottle of vodka. Deliberately, so it seemed, paying no attention to me, the man was calmly slicing circles of an apple into a glass, and then drinking his tea slowly and with enjoyment. So this was Yegor Yakovlevich.

'I can't do it,' he said briefly and with a kind of cold sadness before I had hardly had time even to state my business. I was standing in the doorway and I could either sit down at the table, if he invited me, or settle myself on a wooden couch by the door, which was crammed with boxes, felt boots, flowerpots, and other bits and pieces. There I could sit without invitation, although conversation would be awkward as though across a street.

All the same, I sat down on the couch and put the matter to him again, trying of course to get across that I had heard a lot about his fame as a craftsman. All my trouble about the stove I deliberately tried to present in a humorous light, stressing my helplessness and naivety in such matters.

But he reacted to all this as something quite normal and not in the least interesting. He didn't interrupt me, but seemed to say: 'Go on talking. Whatever you like, as much as you like, it's all the same to me; I'll just carry on drinking my tea.' He didn't even look at me, preferring to look out of the window at the bad weather, the slushy street, the bushes in his garden, the uninviting wetness of the yard, the sight of which is very pleasant when you are sitting drinking tea in your habitual and favourite chair, secure in the warmth of a good reliable stove. Yes, obviously he knew the value of an old man's morning hour for drinking tea and smoking, for easy unhurried peaceful meditation and thought.

I soon began to feel that it was too hot in the kitchen. 'Good publicity', I thought, and added to my exposition yet another servile observation about how warm it was and how good it was to come into such a room from the street.

'No, I shall not take it on', again he interrupted me, moving his glass and saucer to one side and starting to smoke.

'But Yegor Yakovlevich!'

'Yegor Yakovlevich, Yegor Yakovlevich', he mimicked me feebly, with patent disdain for the flattering way I used his name and patronymic. 'I said I can't do it. All right?'

I have to say that neither the chief of a regional or district department of education nor a high-ranking manager with telephones, secretaries and a list of appointments would have spoken to me with such extreme remoteness and lazy arrogance. 'I can't do it, I won't take it on, that's all.' Even the severest and remotest bureaucrat, faced with such a request, would have had to tell me why he could not comply with it.

'Why can't you do it, Yegor Yakovlevich?'

'For the very reason', he replied not raising his voice and not changing his sad and significant intonation. 'For the very reason that there is only one Yegor Yakovlevich, and many demands are made on him by people. I've only got two hands.' He spread out his big bony hands and his wrists showed from the short sleeves of his faded singlet, and he touched his high forehead with his fingers. 'Two hands, one head no more.' These involuntary gestures seemed only to simplify the substance of the matter to conform to the level of my understanding, and showed that Yegor Yakovlevich was far from underestimating his own importance.

'But Yegor Yakovlevich', I dared to suggest, 'Perhaps you have doubts concerning payment – I'd like to say that as far as I'm concerned. . . .'

'No, no, what has payment got to do with it?' he gave a weak and careless wave of his big, heavy hand. 'My remuneration is well known, I'm telling you – I can't take it on. Do one – and another one turns up. Do it for no one, and no one is hurt. Only yesterday a man came here,' he pointed with the cigarette in his left hand to the empty vodka bottle. 'He tried every way to persuade me.'

'But all the same, Yegor Yakovlevich? . . .'

'Can't you understand Russian?' Again he put his heavy wrist to the empty bottle, almost touching the glass with his little finger. 'There was a man here yesterday. . . .'

He pointed out the empty bottle to me with such great conviction, as proof of the presence of a suppliant, that I could not help seeing it as a real human being who, just like me, needed to be in Yegor Yakovlevich's good books.

At this point I made a simple surmise which, I thought, ought to have occurred to me earlier, at the very beginning of the conversation.

'Well, Yegor Yakovlevich', I said resolutely, going up to the table, 'Perhaps as it's a day of rest. . . .' I raised the empty bottle gently by its neck for greater effect.

Yegor Yakovlevich looked up at me, his light blue eyes reddening with age, and the hint of a smile on his lips.

'I don't take it of a morning', and in the tone of his refusal there was not only remoteness, but censure and edification. 'I don't take it of a morning', he repeated even more firmly and leaning on the edge of the table, got up, obviously wanting to make me understand that the audience was over. 'It's true, a man was here yesterday. . . .'

And as for me, I decided that in his eyes I was simply a man like the one standing on the table in the shape of the empty bottle. We were many, but there was only one Yegor Yakovlevich.

He walked me to the passage and, standing at the open door, for some reason or other said the following words to me, perhaps after all touched by my chagrin: 'If I'm passing sometime, perhaps I'll drop in.'

'Please do,' I answered mechanically, at a loss in fact as to why he should do so.

Very distressed, I left. As if I had tried to do something unworthy but had been forestalled, caught in the act. Why, indeed, had I gone to Yegor Yakovlevich, begging him, making up to him, losing my dignity? Let anyone who wants to, do it, not me. But what could I do now? Wait until the headmaster 'personally took it up', until some stovemaker working at the station became free, until my wife – not getting on too well with her mother – arrived having decided she'd rather live in a barn and be with her husband even though nothing was ready?

I became utterly depressed and began to see my situation in the worst possible light; and, as I could not accuse any one person I began to complain about the imperfect way we managed things in general.

We build unique blast-furnaces from hundreds of different kinds of brick, erect buildings for the purpose of commemorating our residence and work on earth, to provide future generations with an image of the grandeur of our deeds and yearnings. But to build a stove, an ordinary stove of the kind most likely known even in Kiev in Old Russia, to build this heating device for the home of cultured workers of the brain, for a teacher of our own language and literature – that is an insoluble problem!

Walking back I developed a completely irrefutable argument along the general lines that such a situation was intolerable and insane. One after another the phrases took shape in my head, now lyrical and full of pathos, now bitingly ironical, inspired with conviction, truth, and clear as the day itself. Soon I was no longer talking with myself but composing a speech which I was going to deliver straight from a platform, or in an interview with a very important person. Or the phrases formed themselves into paragraphs for a newspaper article which hot from the press would fervently and straightforwardly have drawn attention to the needs of the rural intelligentsia. But this was no longer enough for me. I began to touch on the existing methods and forms of teaching, etc. etc. Gradually and unwittingly I was getting further and further away from my stove. I wanted so much to talk to someone about all these things, to communicate my truthful observations and irrefutable conclusions, to repeat aloud the finest passages of my interior monologue, parade quotations as if plucked there and then from memory.

I went back to the major, without any thought of his promise 'to think of something'; just like that. He lived not far from his local headquarters, in a wooden semi-detached house with a porch just like the one next door.

I was told he was already at the office, and there I found him in the same small room, quiet and deserted. He rose to meet me, quickly closing a thick notebook and slipping it into his desk. My face, excited by the long walk and the hard thinking, must have given him the impression I'd been successful.

'Well, how's things?'

I told him about my visit, and everything now appeared in a humorous vein, and to my own surprise I painted a colourful portrait of Yegor Yakovlevich on his high horse, drinking tea and refusing my request. I even showed him how Yegor Yakovlevich gestured towards the bottle: 'There was a man here yesterday. . . .' We both had a good laugh.

'Well', said the major, 'I'll have to build the stove myself.'

'How, I mean. . . .'

'With bricks, of course!' He laughed, showing his big teeth and lifting his hand to his mouth.

Only then, incidentally, did I notice that there was something very attractive and rather touching about his smile. It immediately transformed his preoccupied and melancholy face.

'You mean to say you'll rebuild the stove yourself?'

'Yes. I'd entrust it to my deputy but he wouldn't know how to do it.' Not without satisfaction the major observed my perplexity. 'Tomorrow's Saturday, right? We'll start in the evening.'

It had all turned out so simple, but at the same time a little dodgy. Was it right for the major, from one point of view my superior, to hire himself out as a stovemaker?

'Don't you trust me? Didn't you see the stove when you came to my house? The wife's happy with it.'

'Of course I trust you. To be sure, I'm grateful. But then we must come to an agreement about various things.'

'Like my fee?' he prompted me cheerfully and readily. 'Don't worry, that's no problem. We'll sort something out.'

'Nevertheless. . . .'

'Nevertheless, let's change the subject. It wouldn't do for a district military commandant to earn some extra money building stoves! If such a thing ever reached the authorities. . . .'

'But if they find out that you're just building stoves?'

'Let them. It's none of their business. Look, I sewed all these things'; he brushed his hand over his tunic and breeches. 'I get the cloth and make up the pattern myself. I make all the outdoor clothes for my children. I could do yours too.'

The next evening he arrived at my house with a bundle under his arm, containing some old summer army-trousers and a field shirt, a stovemaker's hammer, a collapsible metal rule, a roll of wire, and some bits of string.

He looked around, inspected the stove and the cooking-range, then took a chair and sat down in the middle of the room facing the stove, and, contemplating it, began to smoke.

'Mmmm . . .' he said after reflecting for a short time.

'What?'

'Nothing. It's going to be very messy.'

'So what? Ivanovna will clear everything away.'

'Have you any wood?' he asked.

'Wood? Yes. What for?'

'To light the stove.'

'You mean when you've built the new one?'

'No, first we must try to light this one.'

Either he was joking or he'd forgotten everything I'd told him about the stove.

'But all you'll succeed in doing is to smoke the place out. Don't you believe me?'

'Yes, of course I do. But we've got to light it. Where's the wood?'

There was wood in the corridor, including some partly charred logs that had already been in the stove.

The major removed his tunic and began work so confidently that I was prepared to contemplate the possibility that Ivanovna and I had overlooked something, thus causing our failure on previous occasions. Now he was about to light the stove, and everything would turn out normal! This would be splendid, but my whole story with the stove would now look preposterous and absurd!

Was I glad when the stove smoked up just as it did with Ivanovna, Fyodor or myself.

'No, comrade major', I said.

'What do you mean, no?'

'It won't burn.'

'Very good! That's what we need.' He laughed. 'What is important is for us to find out why and how it isn't burning.'

The small bits had burnt up; the larger pieces had darkened but not caught; there was smoke everywhere, as usual. The major went outside to look at the chimney. I went out too. It was still light.

How many times after lighting the stove I had run out on to the street, straining to see if any smoke was coming from the chimney. I still remember from childhood I would observe the chimney very closely to know if they had put the samovar on the stove, and the air would begin to tremble above the chimney – now the smoke would appear, and then it would disappear.

The major went back into the house, grabbed a length of string with a heavy metal nut tied to the end and started to climb the ladder to the roof. I watched him up there, lowering the weight into the chimney, moving it around, letting it go deep, and then raising it. It was exactly like rescuing a bucket from a well with a grappling hook.

At that moment a tall man came along the road. He was wearing a jacket with a red fur collar and slanting breast pockets. He stopped and holding his left hand to the peak of his cap stared up at the roof. He had a cane in his right hand. When the major pulled the string out and climbed down the man came closer and I saw that it was Yegor Yakovlevich. He nodded to me and turning to the major, asked:

'Well, how's it going?'

'The devil knows. There's nothing in the pipe, but it still won't burn.'

You'd have thought that they had known each for a long time and that they were working together on this ill-fated stove. We entered the house which was still full of smoke; the two men began discussing the stove. They kept referring to 'him', meaning the unknown craftsman who had built the thing.

'He should be punched in the snout', said the major with gloomy conviction.

But the old stovemaker rejoined in a conciliatory way: 'That wouldn't help. The main thing is he wasn't a stovemaker – maybe he was a cobbler. Linking two flues – from the range and from the stove – was beyond his understanding.' As he said this Yegor Yakovlevich drew his cane around the body of the stove like a pointer, knocking and leaving marks. 'Just a cobbler.'

This was said as if he were comparing the cobbler's trade with something immeasurably more complex, for instance with art, as in Pushkin's line: 'A cobbler once was looking at a painting.'

The two stovemakers stopped for a smoke and went on discussing the question for a long time. They behaved like doctors who have just examined a patient, not in the least embarrassed by the presence of the relatives or friends who only understand fifty per cent of their terminology, their reservations, their shoulder-shrugging, their enigmatic tracings in the air.

'If you don't know how to do it, don't take it on,' concluded Yegor Yakovlevich, not without an allusion, it seemed to me, to those present.

Without taking offence, the major explained. 'Of course I'm not a stovemaker but I needed a stove at home, so I built one. And when a man's in difficulties' – he nodded in my direction – 'he must be helped, somehow.'

'Quite right,' said Yegor Yakovlevich, pleased with the major's modesty. 'But, also, help him so he won't need any further help.'

'Yegor Yakovlevich!' I suddenly felt a new surge of hope. 'Yegor Yakovlevich, that's quite true. So. . . .'

The major supported me to perfection, 'I'd prepare the clay for you, according to your instructions, Yegor Yakovlevich. It would be very valuable for me to work under such a master, honest to God!' He displayed his large toothy smile, covering it with the hand in which he held his cigarettes.

In the end it is the plain ordinary folk who unerringly find their way to the inaccessible hearts of uncommon people.

'Well, what am I to do with you? I must come to your assistance,' said the craftsman, and this 'must come to your assistance' was just like the wording of ordinary resolutions emanating from district or regional headquarters: 'come to the assistance of such and such a department for this or that reason'.

Yegor Yakovlevich sat down on the chair facing the stove, just like the major before him, and staring at it absent-mindedly, muttered into his beard:

'Assistance. Must come to the assistance. . . .' And waving his stick first in the direction of the major, and then towards the stove, said somewhat deliberately and melodiously: 'Well, my dear friend, by tomorrow you will dismantle the stove down to the last brick, and so there won't be any breakage, put the bricks in a pile, understand?'

I noticed that he spoke to the major in a familiar way, already treating him as his subordinate, although he could not have failed to see the tunic hanging on the chair, with its epaulettes, and in this he also resembled the authorities.

The major said he would climb up to the roof straightaway. I of course expressed my readiness to help him, but Yegor Yakovlevich explained that there was no need to go up on the roof.

'This has nothing to do with the chimney-stack; this one will do if it's properly supported.'

Neither I nor the major knew how to do this. So Yegor Yakovlevich took hold of his cane by both ends and explained the task in an exemplary way for the layman, once again addressing himself only to the major:

'Take two bars of wood, as reliable as possible of course, not less than four inches thick. Find the shoulders of the stack in the attic and bang the bars in to prop them up. You can suspend the whole stove, not only the stacks, if you want to. How would you take a stove to pieces on the ground floor if there's another one on top of it on the second floor? Break up both of them for the sake of one? Not on your life, old man. . . .'

And already from these first practical instructions I could see that the old man had good reason to adopt the dominant role. I did not succeed in mentioning payment because with one nod he took his leave and departed. All over the floor were the footprints left by his felt boots and the home-made galoshes made from the inner tube of a motor tyre.

By early evening the major and I had taken the stove apart, leaving the range untouched and propping up the stack in the way he had described. I myself feared that some misfortunes might arise from this propping up but the major coped with the task so confidently that he might have done it many times before. To my eyes he was an altogether fine fellow – the sort you often find in the army, who can do everything and who take on anything fearlessly, acting on the well-known proposition that it's not the gods who bake flowerpots. He made the props we needed out of a sixty-millimetre board, successfully splitting it with an axe, and then smoothing the edges by using the axe like a plane. With his habitual skill he freed the stove-doors and dampers and bolts from under the bricks, and pulled out the wires which fastened them in their sockets. It was easy and pleasant to work with him. He never dispirited his clumsy and unskilful assistant with his superiority. He did not get annoyed and did not make fun of me, though he occasionally made a cheerful joke without any malice. We prepared clay and sand, and made a box for the clay, so that everything would be to hand, and while we were washing and changing our clothes the tea-kettle began to boil on my primus.

'I could do with some tea,' the major conceded. We sat down in the front room, where it was cleaner. We drank our tea, smoked and chatted. The major browsed among the books I had brought in here to protect from the dust, and pointing at a tattered one-volume *Nekrasov* observed that it needed rebinding. And when I said that surely you wouldn't find a good bookbinder round here, he volunteered to bind the book himself, and even to teach me how to do it. Of course it wouldn't be the same without machine-cutting, but at least the book would keep better than before. He loved books with that gently respectful care you find only among the most ordinary readers. He looked right through my pitiful library, examining every volume in turn, lingering most over the poetry. I said that he must be a poetry lover, and that this was not so common among those who, so to speak, were not specialists. He gave a shy and at the same time intrepid smile, emphasized by the joking arrogance in his tone of voice: 'What do you want, I write verse myself. Even publish it!'

'That's great,' I said, and not knowing what to add, asked: 'Excuse me, do you write under a pseudonym? I can't recall seeing your name in print.'

'No, I use my own name. And I don't get published all that often. And when I do, it's in the district paper and in *Soviet Soldier*. You don't see them round here.'

With these words he became somewhat sad, which compelled me to show a greater interest in his poetry. I asked him to show me some, sometime. He agreed at once, and began to recite by heart.

At this juncture I would like to explain that I am not calling the major by his name precisely because he has been published and it would be possible for someone to establish that he and the hero of my story are one and the same person. And most emphatically I would not want that to happen because I am describing him down to the smallest detail, just as in life. I tried to invent a name for him in this story but the whole business sickened me, and nothing suited him anyway, so he remains, simply, 'the major'.

The major recited some of his poems. I do not remember them; they were like the great majority of poems that appear in newspapers and magazines, about the virgin lands, military glory, the struggle for peace, hydro-electric stations, dams, girls, little children – future contemporaries of the communist age – and of course poems about poetry. And they were not just similar through an involuntary similarity of imitation, which the author would have wanted to avoid, but it seemed that his efforts were solely directed towards making him sound like other people, as verses are *supposed* to sound. This I could not discuss with him: I already liked him too much, for his kindness, his comradely sympathy, his jack-of-all-trades skill, and his genuine and unforced modesty. I said something about a not very successful rhyme; it was hardly a significant observation.

'No', he answered quietly, 'My rhyming . . . my rhyming's all right.' And setting the books in a pile on the edge of the table, he repeated thoughtfully: 'My rhyming's all right. . . .' There was a sad incompleteness in his reply: perhaps he himself knew something about his poems that I had not touched on and, it seemed to him, had not understood. And suddenly he began to speak as if in self-justification, and as if to forestall certain valuations and conclusions concerning his poetry: 'You know, I'm not so stupid as to think that this stuff has any sort of merit. But I'm not afraid of work. I'm as stubborn as an ox, and I can go without sleep, food and drink if there's something I have to achieve. I began writing during the war, not while I was with my company, but when I was wounded: one wound, one notebook full of poems; the wound meant creative leave.' He laughed at his own joke and continued: 'And I was lucky: I was wounded four times, not too seriously but not superficially either; just right; a month and a half behind the lines. Read and write to your heart's content – and back to the front. And my luck held out. I have a full day off work every week. Evenings? Nights? They're mine too. And frankly speaking, I can't do without it, whatever I embark on I have to master. I don't give up until it *is* mastered. Like this stove here, you know. Do you think I learned how to be a stovemaker? Took courses in it? But I had to build a stove. There was nobody I could hire. And frankly speaking I couldn't have afforded to hire anyone. There's seven of us, God be blessed. So what did I do? I built it twice. First time I did it in a rough sort of way, heated it up, figured out where its secret was hidden and then took it to pieces, as we did with this one – that one wasn't completely dry of course – and then put it together again. It heats all right. Maybe Yegor Yakovlevich would find something wrong with it, but it works.' And he laughed again, but somewhat ambiguously. There was an element of boastfulness in his daring, but also a readiness to admit just how funny the whole thing was.

During our conversation it turned out that we had been on neighbouring fronts, and this highly provisional condition of being neighbours in the past brought us closer together, as if we had lived in the same remote neighbourhood.

I walked him home part of the way, then took a long time to fall asleep in my cold and dusty room with the dismantled stove. The thought occurred to me that this nice man, busy in the service and with a large family on his hands, ought not to exhaust himself writing verse. It was clear to me that his verse was not in fact the expression of a deep inner need that had to be articulated in this particular artistic mode. It was not necessary to have spent four years at the front and be wounded four times to write about the war as he did. In his verses about the children of socialism the author – father of five children – was completely absent; in his poem about the development of the virgin lands I only remember 'bring to the boil/ the virgin soil'; finally in the poems about poetry there was only the repetition of the simple truth that poetry is needed in battle and toil.

Perhaps he wrote all these things only because he was well aware of his capacity to master a new activity, not only without special training but even without an inner compulsion. But no, the urge to be a writer was very highly developed in him; there was no doubt that on this particular road no little disappointment and bitterness awaited him. . . . I was wakened by a knocking on the window above my head, the softly insistent tapping of a stick. It was Yegor Yakovlevich, even though it was still very dark outside. I switched on the light and let him in. He was wearing the same jacket with the fur collar, and carrying the same stick. He had no tools and no overalls. While I dressed and generally put things in order, he smoked and coughed, blew his nose and spat, and examined everything that had been left in readiness for the day's work.

'I see – still asleep. I see,' he said in between his coughing and his nose-blowing.

It was obvious that he was very pleased to find me in bed and to arrive before the major whom, by now, I felt I ought to collect. But the major was not more than ten minutes behind the old man.

'It *is* a day off,' he pleaded with a smile, unfolding his bundle of working clothes.

'It may be a day off for some, but for you and me it's a working day,' the old man replied coldly, and this time formally, as the major was still in his tunic with the shoulder-pieces. But perhaps the words were also being addressed to me. 'So you didn't wet the clay last night – pity. More for us to mix now. And wouldn't do any harm to have some warm water. Not for the sake of our hands, but so the mixture sticks better.' He always described the clay and sand as the 'mixture', likening it to cement. Grunting, he squatted before the foundation of the wrecked stove, measured it with his stick and said: 'Four by four. Won't need any more.'

'Yegor Yakovlevich,' the major proffered his folding rule.

The old man waved his stick.

'I have all the measurements we need here. If you don't believe me you can re-measure it.'

But we didn't. It was resolved simply that the foundation of the stove would be four bricks long by four bricks wide. Yegor Yakovlevich shifted his cane to his left hand and quickly with his right laid out the bricks on the dry part, on a marked square, without clay; then he stood up and pointed at them with his stick.

'That is how you will lay them.' Then from the box he took a lump of the clay the major and I had mixed, kneaded it in his hand, frowned and threw it back. 'More sand needed. Hold it! I said a little! That's enough. Give it a good mix.'

We set to work, and from the very beginning each of us had his own well-defined task. I mixed the clay and carried and passed the bricks, the major did the brick-laying and Yegor Yakovlevich – to be precise – placed himself at the head of everything and directed us, as before using his stick as a pointer, sitting down, standing up, smoking and coughing. At times he appeared to be distracted from the stove and held forth didactically and in great detail concerning the benefits of early rising, the necessity for abstention from wine before work, his cough which was particularly bad in the morning, the qualities of bricks from different kilns and of many other materials. But I observed that even so he followed the work closely, so that every brick was laid under the control of his vigilant gaze and with the occasional, apparently chance tap of his stick. Yegor Yakovlevich was clad in his warm jacket but the major and I, in our old working clothes, old field shirts, were already getting a bit too hot for comfort, and mopping our foreheads and noses on our sleeves and cuffs. Our hands were soiled. Yegor Yakovlevich noticed this and did not fail to seize the opportunity for some professional edification.

'Stop for a break, friend. Have a smoke.' With crafty cordiality he offered the major his packet of *Sever* cigarettes. The major drew himself up and held out his hands helplessly. 'Aha! No hands? Got to wash them? Yes? That means you're not a stovemaker yet, only a clay-mixer.' He thrust a cigarette in the major's mouth, gave him a light, and continued: 'Why should I have both hands in the mixture? No, only one, the right one, and my left ought to be in the dry. Look.' He pushed the major aside with his stick, put it on one side, and with only a slight movement of his hands upwards and turning back the sleeves of his jacket, took the next brick with his left hand, dipped his right hand into the pail of water and seized a small piece of clay. 'Look, with the left I place the brick, with the right I smear and clean, understand?' He quickly laid a row of bricks, and although he became slightly out of breath it was obvious that in this business he expended a lot less energy than the major. 'The left hand always in the dry! And it's not only that I can smoke freely and dry myself, but it means the work is cleaner too. If it's a nail you need, here's the nail; your glasses or whatever. To unbutton something or button it up – there.' He showed us how he could do all these things with his left hand. 'But you stand there like some scarecrow in an allotment.'

The master craftsman allowed himself a smile, very satisfied with his lesson and therefore allowing his last words to be taken as a joke. I was very happy for the major; he was not only not offended, but with a rapt smile followed the instructions and demonstration, covering his mouth with his hand held at a small distance so as not to dirty himself.

He wanted to do things the same way as Yegor Yakovlevich, but for some reason soon had to shift a brick from his left hand to his right, and gave up.

'No, Yegor Yakovlevich, you must let me do it my own way.'

'All right. All right,' agreed the old man. 'Rome wasn't built in a day. There are actual stovemakers who have been doing it all their lives, not bad craftsmen at all, who are no worse than you.'

I am sure he would have been pained and displeased if the major had succeeded in adopting his style immediately. Perhaps the major realized this and did not attempt to compete. Then Yegor Yakovlevich, having apparently acquired a taste for teaching, placed two bricks next to each other right at the edge of the stove, and raising his hand over them, as if about to pick them up suggested: 'There, lift them up with one hand.'

But the major burst out laughing and wagged his finger at Yegor Yakovlevich. 'Oh no. That's an old trick. You can't fool me.'

'You know it? That's more like it! Some try as hard as they can, and can't do it. They've bet me bottles of vodka on it.'

As I thought, the trick was to slip your index finger unnoticed between the bricks, then you could easily lift up both bricks at once and move them about.

The reminder of vodka compelled me to start thinking about organizing breakfast, all the more so as it was about 9 o'clock, and completely light. I said that I had to go out for a little while, and went to the station where I bought bread, sausage, tins and vodka at a stall. On the return journey I dropped in at Ivanovna's and was given by her a whole basin of salted cucumbers, which in the fresh air gave off a rare and tasty smell of garlic and fennel. I was glad to have the opportunity to straighten up and stretch my legs. My back was hurting from the work, and I supposed that the major would have a break while I was away. But when I got back I saw that work had gone on without interruption, the laying had already reached the level of the cooking-range, the doors were already done, and Yegor Yakovlevich had taken off his jacket and, in his knitted jersey was laying the first half-circle of the arch, and the major had taken my place and was handing him bricks. They were working quickly and well; the major could hardly match the old man's pace; and they were arguing.

'A man ought to have just one talent,' said Yegor Yakovlevich, managing in such a way that his left hand remained 'in the dry'.

His body, wrapped tightly in the jersey, seemed almost puny compared with his big, long, heavy-wristed arms which were like the claws of a crawfish. Their argument had obviously developed from what they were saying when I was with them earlier – craftsmanship and styles of work, but it had already gone far beyond its original limits.

'One talent. That's all. And if you haven't got a talent, don't take the thing up. Don't spoil things. That's what I always say. Don't you forget it.'

'But why just one?' retorted the major, peacefully and with an air of superiority. 'The Renaissance? Yes, the Renaissance. Leonardo da Vinci.'

Yegor Yakovlevich was obviously hearing these names for the first time in his life and was angry that he did not know them, but he did not want to give way.

'None of us knows anything about that; we don't know what went on then.'

'We don't know, Yegor Yakovlevich?' said the major, amazed, looking round at me. 'Everyone knows that Leonardo was an artist, a sculptor, an inventor and a writer too. Ask the lad.'

I was obliged to confirm that that really was the case.

'So? He was,' replied the old man angrily, with his back to the wall. 'But when? In days of old . . . when each man was his own reaper, tailor and piper – a jack-of-all trades.'

'Is that a dig at me?'

'No. I'm speaking in general terms. There are new developments, new techniques. Everything's different, old chap.'

I was really amazed at Yegor Yakovlevich's historical approach, and saying this aloud, interrupted the argument with an invitation to eat. At table Yegor Yakovlevich refused point blank to drink.

'Later, when we light the stove. . . . But you have a drink,' he said to the major. 'It doesn't matter for you.'

'But won't you, all the same?'

'No I can't. Not at work. There's no one to do the thinking for me.'

The major did not insist; nor was he offended.

'Well, I'll have a glass. Good health!'

The major and I had a drink. The conversation again turned to literature. We touched on Mayakovsky, about whom the major spoke adoringly, now and then reciting his verses by heart with such enthusiasm that he even forgot to cover his smile with his hand. And I wondered why someone with such a love for Mayakovsky could himself write so differently, so evenly, the absolute opposite to Mayakovsky, imitating everything on earth except his idol. But I didn't ask him about this and said only that acquainting my pupils with the poetry of Mayakovsky often brought me up against words and locutions which went against the rules of our native tongue as it had been taught to us. The major retorted hotly, almost angrily, calling me in a joking way a conservative and dogmatist.

Yegor Yakovlevich ate languidly, sipped tea, and smoked in silence, haughty and alienated, waiting for our conversation to end. 'If I haven't heard anything about this, and know nothing' – his expression, amid coughs and puffs, seemed to say – 'it's because all this is useless and without interest for me, and certainly is a lot of nonsense.' But when we mentioned Pushkin, he said:

'Pushkin is a great Russian poet,' and he said it as if he were the only one to know it, had reached this conclusion through his own intellect, and was the first person in the whole wide world to say so. 'Oh, what a great poet', and screwing up his eyes he too recited with an exaggerated expression of tender emotion and feeling:

> Tell me, uncle, it wasn't a vain chance
> That Moscow, burning, surrendered to France.

'But that's Lermontov', laughed the major; but the old man threw him a glance and continued:

> There were some battles, eh,
> And *what* battles, they say.

'But that's Lermontov's *Borodino*.' The major interrupted him with cheerful indignation and nudged me with his elbow:

> All Russia recalls with good reason O
> The day of Borodino.

Yegor Yakovlevich pronounced the last word loudly, distinctly, and even poked his finger at the major: 'I', it said, 'know what you're talking about. And can speak too.' And, obviously determined not to be interrupted, continued: 'Ah, and *The Battle of Poltava*: "The East is glowing with a new dawn. . . ."'

'That's Pushkin. Quite true.' The major did not give up. 'Only it's part of a complete poem called *Poltava*. But it is Pushkin.'

'And did I say it wasn't Pushkin? Who else could have written it? Mayakovsky? Not on your life, old chap.'

'Mayakovsky's dead now. We don't know what he might have written if he'd lived.'

'Yah.' The old man waved his heavy hand, completely distrustful. 'Yah.'

'Well, you're a mule, Yegor Yakovlevich.' The major shook his head worriedly and moved the wrinkles of his forehead up to the very roots of his thick black crop of hair. 'A real mule.'

It was evidently a great pleasure for the old man to be told that he was a mule, but immediately he made clear that this was not exactly new to him.

'Well, I'm over seventy, thank the Lord. When you reach my age, then you can speak.' This referred not only to the major, but to me and to the whole of our generation.

But even at this moment the major could not resist a small but triumphant celebration of his superiority:

'A mule. A mule. But *Borodino* was, all the same, written by Lermontov.'

Yegor Yakovlevich said nothing and, thanking me, got up from the table noticeably depressed. I think he himself realized he had blundered over *Borodino*. But it would have been as painful a wound for him to admit this as to admit he had never heard of Leonardo da Vinci. I was sorry for him, as one is always sorry for an old man compelled to undergo defeat by those with the advantage of youth, knowledge and a good memory.

After breakfast work proceeded merrily apace. Both stovemakers began laying the bricks: Yegor Yakovlevich, on the kitchen side, the major in the other room, and me in my own position – of working for both of them. But work went ahead in silence, except for brief comments strictly pertaining to the job in hand. Perhaps this was a consequence of their recent differences, in which the major clearly came out on top, but perhaps the very laying was becoming more complicated: various mechanisms, vents, bends, the connecting of the stove to the main flue – all this demanded particular concentration.

I did not try to draw the stovemakers out of their silence because I hardly had time even to supply them with the materials they needed. And when they stopped for a smoke I hurried to prepare and organize everything they needed, in order to make things easier for myself. The body of the new stove had now risen to the hole in the ceiling, where the old chimney stack was suspended, and being less voluminous than its predecessor, appeared somehow unusual, even smart. The heating walls of the stove, and the mirror, were laid out, all a quarter of a brick thick, that is, one brick standing on its edge. When Yegor Yakovlevich began to make from the bricks a vent under the ceiling, like a cornice, the stove became even more beautiful: in my mind's eye I already saw it whitewashed; it would be a fine adornment to the room when everything had been cleaned up and tidied in readiness for Lyolya's arrival. The only question was, would it heat up as it should.

For the work at the top some sort of scaffolding was necessary, and we used the stools and then the table, which we covered anyhow with newspapers. Only Yegor Yakovlevich worked up top there now, and he was indeed king of the castle.

When he needed some bricks for the cornice with a quarter knocked off, that is with a smoothly chopped-off corner, he ordered the major to do this. The major spoiled one, and then another, and looking hot and bothered attempted a third, but that one split into three parts. I anticipated some impatient and caustic remarks from Yegor Yakovlevich but he seemed to view his assistant's failure with sympathy:

'Trashy brick. Call this a brick? Give it here.'

He grasped the brick skilfully with his left hand which was still in the dry, threw it up, catching it in his palm and gently tapping as though it were one egg on top of another, shaped it the way he wanted with the hammer. He did the same with a second brick, and a third, and with all the bricks, only for some of them he needed not one but two or more taps.

'Yes,' said the major. 'That's the way. Ye gods!'

But the old craftsman wanted to be magnanimous. He attributed his enviable dexterity to the varied quality of the bricks.

'You never know when you're going to be lucky.' However he could restrain a cunning smile. 'Incredible how many turned out O.K. . . .'

The major and I burst out laughing, and Yegor Yakovlevich himself laughed, and I could see that he was more than compensated for his defeat in the other sphere. We both supplied him with what he needed, and we had to admire the way he placed brick after brick under the edge of the old chimney stack, and how afterwards the temporary shoulder-bars were knocked out from under it, and nothing terrible happened, and everything was perfectly measured though Yegor Yakovlevich had not once used a rule.

Twilight was already darkening the room when Yegor Yakovlevich grunting climbed down from his scaffolding and the triumphant moment of trying out the new stove had arrived. I wanted to switch on the light but Yegor Yakovlevich protested.

'No reason. Won't the stove be good enough for you?'

He dropped before the stove, but this time kneeling not squatting, sitting on the backs on his huge felt boots, as peasants generally sit on a sledge, by bonfires or around a cauldron on the ground. Ranging some light splinters on the still damp grating, he struck a match but did not immediately apply it; first he lit some shreds of newspaper and thrust them through the small door of the ash-pit below and only then poked the match, which had burned right down to his finger-nails and curled like a hook, under the fine curly shavings. The paper burned quickly in the ash-pit, but in the stove the fire burned slowly, weakly. I was afraid to breathe as I watched it, but it caught. We all three looked at it in complete silence. And it burned more and more merrily, enveloping the small bits of wood more and more strongly. Yes, to begin with, it had been like that with the old stove: what would happen next? Yegor Yakovlevich began piling on firewood, arranging it like Ivanovna did; the fire caught on more decisively and vividly, further and further; more and more, the stove blazed up brightly and gaily, and it was particularly beautiful and pleasant in the twilight that was flooding the room. Yegor Yakovlevich rose heavily from his knees.

'Well, congratulations on your new stove', he said and began to wash his hands in the bucket we had been using for work.

So that was why he didn't let me switch the light on: the fire in the stove would be more visible, look more beautiful. Yegor Yakovlevich was a poet in his trade.

When the major and I had washed and changed our clothes, not without anxiety I finally raised the question of what payment Yegor Yakovlevich would want. 'The payment I expect is well known.' I remembered his words and was ready for anything, but I was afraid because I did not know if I had the ready cash to settle things on the spot. The stove was burning really well, the big logs had already been put on and they had caught fire, and everything was going so swimmingly that I forgot to run out and see if the smoke was coming out of the chimney. But it would be since the stove wasn't smoking the room out.

'Oh why talk about that.' Somehow Yegor Yakovlevich brushed the question aside. 'Why talk about that?'

'No, Yegor Yakovlevich. I'm asking you to tell me how much I owe you.'

'Well, what he gets' – he pointed at the major, 'I get.' The tone of his reply as before was semi-serious, semi-joking. 'We worked together. And you too ought to get your share: you helped us.'

'Yegor Yakovlevich,' the major cut in, 'We're here on completely different terms. Nothing is due to me. I said in advance that I would take nothing, in as much as I'm not a specialist.'

'And I shall take nothing, because I am a specialist. Understand? No more discussion! But, on the occasion of the launching of the new stove . . . I won't refuse a. . . .'

I tried to lie that, as a matter of fact, the payment would not be a burden to me, that the school would pay the greater part of the sum, but at this point Yegor Yakovlevich interrupted me sternly and touchily:

'That's the worst thing you could have said. Take money from the school? I'm not that poor, thank God . . . I'll not allow that. . . .'

Maybe his touchiness was a result of his annoyance that the major had again forestalled him in this matter by refusing payment in advance, but in any event I had to bring this particular conversation to an end.

The major heard all this and, when we were sitting at table, stared at Yegor Yakovlevich with a kind of strange, cheerful and also embarrassed look; looked and looked; then suddenly asked:

'Yegor Yakovlevich, are you angry with me about something?' The question was unusual if only because the major addressed the old man in a familiar way. 'Well, maybe I offended you or something?'

'No, why do you ask?' He answered with a tone of surprise and as if seeing him for the first time, in his turn stared at the major in his tunic with the shoulder-pieces and the three rows of medals and ribbons.

'How could you offend me? We worked together. It all went well. No reason for us to quarrel. . . .'

Yegor Yakovlevich was now addressing the major formally; apparently he considered that the latter was not now subordinate to him as he had been during work.

'All right, you win. You're a good fellow, Yegor Yakovlevich. And a master of your craft too. Let's have a drink. Good health!'

'Good health to you too!'

They clinked glasses as if there had indeed been something between them, and now there was reconciliation and mutual joy.

Then Ivanovna knocked on the door. She had seen smoke coming out of the chimney, and Fyodor dragged himself after her; they too had a drink with us, praised the stove and praised Yegor Yakovlevich to his face. He drank three glasses, grew red in the face, and boasted that he could build not only ordinary Russian or Dutch stoves, but Swedish ones and a round *burak*, and a fireplace, and a stove that worked on steam, and that no one else could do it as well as he because he had talent and talent is uncommon. Perhaps he became a little tedious, unpleasantly loud, but when I wanted to pour him another, he covered the glass firmly with his hand: 'That's my lot.' And started saying goodbye.

I volunteered to go with him, not only because he was obviously drunk, but also because I hoped to arrange payment with him on the way. But he thanked me ceremoniously for the entertainment, found his stick, and took his leave.

'Go with me? I'm not a young girl. . . .'

'What a mule,' said the major after him.

We sat there and chatted on. Ivanovna brought in new wood for tomorrow's fire and started clearing up the mess. The stove got dry and even warmed the room a little, and I felt so good in body and soul that it seemed impossible I should have to face any more trials and tribulations for the rest of my life.

(1953–58)

OHIO UNIVERSITY LIBRARY

Please return this book as soon as you have finished with it. In order to avoid a fine it must be returned by the latest date stamped below.

NOV 23 1975
NOV 24 1975

RETURN BY

NOV 5 1985

JUN 1 6 1997
JUN 1 0 1997

CF